CHILD CARE LAW

A SUMMARY

SCOTLAND

Rhona Pollock

coram BAAF
adoption • fostering • kinship

Published by
CoramBAAF Adoption and Fostering Academy
41 Brunswick Square
London WC1N 1AZ
www.corambaaf.org.uk

Coram Academy Limited registered as a company limited by guarantee in England and Wales number 9697712, part of the Coram group, charity number 312278

British Library Cataloguing in Publication Data
A catalogue record for this book is available
from the British Library

ISBN 978 1 913384 37 1

Project management by Jo Francis, Publications, CoramBAAF
Designed and typeset by Helen Joubert Design
Printed in Great Britain by Lavenham Press
Trade distribution by Turnaround Publisher Services, Unit 3, Olympia Trading Estate, Coburg Road, London N22 6TZ

Contents

Note about the author

Rhona Pollock is a Scottish solicitor who has worked in the private and public sectors in London and Scotland since 1986. She was a Children's Reporter for 20 years; a panel practice adviser and trainer for Children's Hearings Scotland; a legal consultant for BAAF/CoramBAAF; and in 2015 (with five colleagues) set up the Scottish charity now known as the Association for Fostering, Kinship and Adoption (AFKA) Scotland, where she was the legal consultant until 2025. She was also the legal consultant for the Kinship Care Advice Service Scotland. Rhona is currently Admissions Manager at the Law Society of Scotland, as well as Safeguarder to the Children's Hearing, Child Welfare Reporter to the Courts, and Legally Qualified Member of SSSC.

Acknowledgements

I should like to thank my dedicated colleagues past and present, AFKA Scotland members, and all those who have given me the benefit of their knowledge, insight and experience; they have taught me so much and supported me throughout my career. I am also grateful to Jo Francis in CoramBAAF's Publications Department in London for her patience and advice. Thanks too to Emma Letham, Senior Associate at Anderson Strathearn, Solicitors, for her reviewing the text.

This book is dedicated to my daughters, Hannah and Romy,
who make everything worthwhile.

Preface

This book is the revised edition of *Child Care Law: A summary of the law in Scotland*. It takes account of the changes since the previous edition in 2014, particularly those arising from the Children and Young People (Scotland) Act 2014; the Age of Criminal Responsibility (Scotland) Act 2019; the Children (Scotland) Act 2020; and the UNCRC (Incorporation) (Scotland) Act 2024; and various amendments to existing primary and secondary legislation along with supporting regulations, court rules and guidance.

The **UNCRC (Incorporation) (Scotland) Act 2024** received Royal Assent on 16 January 2024, and most of its provisions came into force on 16 July 2024. It places children's rights at the centre of the making and implementation of laws and will potentially have a wide-ranging impact on child care matters. At the time of writing, subordinate legislation and guidance are not available.

The Promise[1] has fundamentally changed our approach to looked after children. It is a commitment made by Scotland to care experienced children and young people that they will grow up loved, safe and respected. The Promise was made in February 2020 following the Independent Care Review, which found that the current "care system" was not working. It focuses on empowering voice, influencing culture and language, and creating a good childhood, not a system. The Promise implementation plan sets out actions and commitments to Keep the Promise for care experienced children, young people, and their families. The Promise Scotland supports Scotland's promise to care experienced people and helps people and organisations across Scotland to keep the Promise.

The **Children (Care and Justice) (Scotland) Act 2024** focuses on children who come into conflict with the law and will inevitably make changes to the

1 https://thepromise.scot/

children's hearings system (Scotland's care and justice system for children in Scotland).

As with previous editions, this book is not a detailed legal textbook about what is a wide-reaching area of law. Rather, it aims to provide a basic framework of the law for those who do not need to know more *and* a starting point for those who have to look further. Any factual mistakes and any expressed opinions are, of course, mine.

Statutory references are given throughout the text with abbreviations listed in Chapter 1. There is a list of further reading and useful websites.

The following is my understanding of the law as at April 2025.

Rhona Pollock

1

Introduction, some definitions and abbreviations

This chapter sets out the main legislative background for child care law in Scotland, and other relevant provisions. It includes an outline of devolution, and significant legislation. It also gives abbreviations for legislation, regulations and guidance and other terms used in the text. Acts, regulations and court rules are listed in date order.

1 Statutory background

Many provisions given here are referred to in more detail in later chapters. Others are relevant to the general application of the law, such as the Human Rights Act 1998.

2 Scots law and devolution

2.1

The **Scotland Act 1998 (the 1998 Act)** established the Scottish Parliament, Holyrood, from July 1999. As a result, Acts operational in Scotland may either be passed by the Westminster Parliament or by Holyrood. Those dated before 1999 will have derived from Westminster, while those passed after 1999 could be from either Parliament. Acts with 'Scotland' (or a clear reference to Scotland) in their title apply to Scotland, but in other Acts, it is necessary to check the 'Extent' section near the end to find out if they apply to Scotland.

The effect of the 1998 Act and devolution is that devolved matters may be legislated for in Scotland, but this does not mean that differences from the rest of the UK only arise because of the 1998 Act. Scots law and the Scottish legal system have always been distinct from those in the rest of the UK. This is particularly so in relation to children and how children are protected and supported in Scotland. For example, in 2019 the defence of reasonable chastisement (where parents use physical force to discipline their children) was abolished in Scotland, but not in England.

2.2 Children (Equal Protection from Assault) (Scotland) Act 2019

Most aspects of day-to-day life come under devolved powers, such as education, social work, health services, local authorities, property law, family law, the police and criminal law. Retained matters, which Holyrood cannot usually pass laws about, include the benefits system, immigration law, employment law, defence, foreign affairs and anti-discrimination law. Holyrood cannot change the basic rules about them, but it can legislate to implement policy and practice in these areas. Conversely, Holyrood can “give back” to Westminster the power to make law on devolved matters, if Members of Scottish Parliament (MSPs) vote for this in a Sewel motion. For example, Holyrood allowed the Adoption and Children Act 2002 to include some provisions for Scotland, although most of the Act does not apply in Scotland. Also, the Civil Partnership Act 2004, passed by Westminster, was allowed to include devolved issues as well as retained ones, so that it covers the whole of the UK, albeit that there are substantial Scottish provisions.

The parameters of this were explored by the Supreme Court in 2021, as mentioned below.

3 Limitations to the powers of the Scottish Parliament

3.1

Holyrood can only legislate about "devolved" matters, not about anything that is "reserved" to Westminster. But the 1998 Act states that unless a matter listed in it is reserved to Westminster, it is devolved to Holyrood.

A judgement by the Supreme Court in 2021 made clear that the Scottish Parliament cannot pass any laws that affect the UK Parliament's power to legislate for Scotland – not just in reserved areas of law but also in devolved areas. Any provision that seeks to do so falls outwith the legislative competence of the Scottish Parliament; it cannot be left to the Scottish courts to impose qualifications upon the provision on individual cases.

REFERENCE by the Attorney General and the Advocate General for Scotland – European Charter of Local Self-Government (Incorporation) (Scotland) Bill [2021] UKSC 42

4 Influence in Scotland of other jurisdictions' practice

Many of the principles around adoption, kinship care and fostering are similar to those in England, Wales and Northern Ireland, and sheriffs and judges will, at times, refer to decisions made by courts in those jurisdictions. Research, learning and best practice are developed around the UK and are shared and adapted within the four nations. Nevertheless, primary and secondary legislation and Scottish Government guidance mean that the legal landscape within Scotland remains definitively Scottish.

5 The United Nations Convention on the Rights of the Child (UNCRC)

The Convention has 54 articles that cover all aspects of a child's life and set out the civil, political, economic, social and cultural rights that all children, everywhere, are entitled to receive. It sets out how organisations within States must work together to make sure all children can enjoy all their rights. It is a simple promise to every child that they are entitled to the best possible start in life, to an education, to a safe place to live, to quality health care and to protection from harm.

It is the most widely ratified treaty in the world with the UK ratifying it in 1991, but it has not yet been made part of domestic law in the UK, except for Scotland. This means that many of the protections contained within it have not yet been accessible to children and young people in Scotland, with no prospect of that happening across the rest of the UK.

Incorporation of the UNCRC into Scots Law

In January 2024, the Scottish Parliament unanimously passed legislation making Scotland the first UK nation to incorporate the UNCRC in domestic law, endeavouring to respect, protect and fulfil children's rights. This became operational in July 2024.

https://www.legislation.gov.uk/asp/2024/1/contents/enacted

It contains several measures that empower children in realising their rights:

- There is a "compatibility duty" that makes it unlawful for public authorities, including Scottish Government Ministers, to act incompatibly with Acts of the Scottish Parliament. If a breach occurs, children and their representatives can use the courts to enforce their rights.
- It contains specific measures to remove barriers that children and young people may face in realising their rights and accessing justice, including bringing proceedings against the authority in any civil court or tribunal which has jurisdiction to grant. Where the court/tribunal finds the act or proposed act to be unlawful, it may grant such relief or remedy, or make such order as it considers effective, just and appropriate. Where the court awards damages and in deciding on the amount, it must consider whether this is necessary to provide just satisfaction to the person to whom the award would be made.
- Where it is a child bringing proceedings and seeking remedy, the child must have an opportunity to express their views about the effectiveness of that relief, remedy or order and consideration must be given to their views.
- It will be up to the Scottish Government to present a Children's Rights Scheme before the Scottish Parliament, setting out arrangements for

fulfilling the compatibility duty under the Act and to report on the actions taken and future plans for children's rights.

- There is an obligation on the Scottish Government to conduct a Child Rights Impact Assessment on every new policy and legislation that affects children to ensure that children's rights are upheld when considering new policy and fiscal decisions.

The legislation demonstrates a commitment by the Scottish Parliament towards children for them to survive, thrive and reach their full potential as envisaged under the Convention. It allows a mechanism for children to challenge any obstacle to their exercising their rights under the Convention.

Once any secondary legislation is passed and guidance issued, the reality of this aspiration will be clearer.

6 The Promise

A significant element of Scotland's committed approach to looked after children and those living apart from birth parents is contained within The Promise.

In 2016, the Scottish Government appointed an Independent Review of the looked after system and their findings were published in 2020. Consequently, the Scottish Government issued a Promise to the children of Scotland that Scotland would protect and love its children. In 2022, the Scottish Government published an Implementation Plan setting out what they will do to keep The Promise by 2030. The introduction to Holyrood of legislation enshrining this principle was enacted under the Children (Care and Justice) (Scotland) Act 2024. Public bodies, local authorities and charities have made sure these principles underpin their policies and practice.

7 Scottish criminal and civil law and private law

There is a distinction between criminal and civil law. Criminal law is self-explanatory and, for the purposes of this book, anything that is not criminal is treated as civil. The children's hearing system straddles civil and criminal law and has been described as a *sui generis* system, that is, of its own kind, unique.

WW v Kennedy 1988 SCLR 236 at 239

8 Private and public law

Another distinction is made between private and public law. Private law relates to matters between private individuals and their rights and responsibilities in relation to one other. Public law deals with the ways in which society and the state become involved in the lives of children and families. Adoption law straddles this divide, as it is a private law action in the courts, but often (not always) comes about because of public law intervention by a local authority.

9 Local authority

"Local authority" is defined in the 1995 and 2007 Acts as meaning the whole local authority and all its departments, not just the social work department. It means that the various departments within the local authority are obliged to carry out responsibilities, duties, etc, when they are required by children and families, whether the children are "in need", "looked after" or requiring other services. The 2011 Act does not have a specific definition of the words "local authority", but it should be taken to mean the same as in the 1995 Act. In addition, all children who are subject to compulsory supervision orders are "looked after" in terms of the 1995 Act, so its definition applies.

s.93(1) 1995 Act; s.119(1) 2007 Act; s.17(6) 1995 Act as amended by the 2011 Act, Schedule 5, para 2(4)

10 Corporate parents

The term 'corporate parents' was defined in the 2014 Act; corporate parenting is 'the formal and local partnerships between all services responsible for working together to meet the needs of looked after children, young people and care leavers'. There is a statutory responsibility for them to (as far as is reasonably practicable) collaborate with one another to safeguard and promote the wellbeing of looked after children and young people in continuing care or after care as defined by the Act.

s.60 Children and Young People (Scotland) Act 2014

Guidance provides further information in terms of expectations on corporate parents. Their role should complement and support the actions of parents, families and carers, working with these key adults to deliver positive change for vulnerable children.

https://www.gov.scot/publications/statutory-guidance-part-9-corporate-parenting-children-young-people-scotland/

Good co-operative working among all individuals and agencies making decisions about children or working with them and their families is positively encouraged by the 1995 Act, in private and public law cases, and this has continued under subsequent legislation, including the 2014 Act. There is an expectation that children's parents will work with them and together in decision making about their welfare, even if the parents themselves do not get on. There is an expectation that, where the local authority is involved with children and families, they will work co-operatively and in partnership with them.

11 Conventions and Acts of Parliament

European Convention on Human Rights 1950 **ECHR**

(See the Human Rights Act 1998 below.)

UN Convention on the Rights of the Child 1989 **UNCRC**

Until 2024 this had not been incorporated into Scots law and was persuasive only. Nonetheless, the Children and Young People (Scotland) Act 2014 placed duties on the Scottish Ministers to consider steps that might achieve 'better or further effect' of the UNCRC and promote public awareness of it. See below (and the Preface) for more information on the 2014 Act. The United Nations Convention on the Rights of the Child (Incorporation) (Scotland) Act 2024 strengthened this commitment by incorporating it into Scottish legislation.

Hague Convention on Protection of Children and Co-operation in Respect of Intercountry Adoption 1993 **Hague Convention**

Governs arrangements for foreign adoption between those countries that have ratified it, including the UK.

Foster Children (Scotland) Act 1984 **1984 Act**

There is also Scottish Government Guidance issued in 2013 – see following chapters on private arrangements and on fostering and kinship care.

Age of Legal Capacity (Scotland) Act 1991 **1991 Act**

Sets out the ages at which children and young people attain legal capacity in civil matters. See Chapter 2.

Children (Scotland) Act 1995 **1995 Act**

Remains one of the primary pieces of legislation providing the range and scope of local authority intervention in the lives of children and their families. The duties of the local authority within this legislation are, in the main, discharged by statutory social work services.

It sets out the fundamental obligations of local authorities, parental responsibilities and rights (PRRs) and the rights of children and young people. It refers to the care, welfare and protection of children and young people up to the age of 16 or 18 depending on the child's legal status. Where the child is a looked after child, the local authority has enhanced duties, including to safeguard and promote the child's welfare which shall be their paramount concern, and to make such use of services available for children cared for by their own parents as appear to the authority reasonable in the child's case.

The Act also permits the local authority to request help, in the exercise of their functions in children's services, from a range of persons and imposes an obligation on the person requested to provide help, unless where doing so would not be compatible with that person's own statutory or other duties.

NB The Act originally amended the 1978 Act, but those provisions (and ss.86–89 about parental responsibilities orders) were replaced by the Adoption and Children (Scotland) Act 2007 (see below). The provisions for the children's hearing system were replaced by the Children's Hearings (Scotland) Act 2011 (see below).

Human Rights Act 1998 **1998 Act**

Incorporated into UK law the rights contained in the European Convention on Human Rights. It means that remedy for breach of a Convention right can be sought in UK courts, without the need to go to the European Court of Human Rights (ECHR).

It is unlawful for a public body to act in a way that is incompatible with the Convention, unless primary legislation leaves no other choice. Courts must, as far as possible, interpret legislation in a way that is compatible with Convention rights.

Adoption (Intercountry Aspects) Act 1999 **1999 Act**

The **vehicle by which the UK implemented the Hague Convention on Intercountry Adoption.** It also made provision about adoptions from countries that are not signed up to the Hague Convention. While much of it has been replaced for Scotland by the Adoption and Children (Scotland) Act 2007, it is still relevant, particularly for adoptions from Hague Convention countries.

Regulation of Care (Scotland) Act 2001 **2001 Act**

Established a system for regulation, registration and inspection of a wide range of care services. It set up the Scottish Commission for the Regulation of Care – the Care Commission – and the Scottish Social Services Council. The provisions of the Act about the Care Commission were replaced by the Public Services Reform (Scotland) Act 2010.

Foster Children (Scotland) Act 1984 **1984 Act**

There is also Scottish Government guidance issued in 2013 – see following chapters on private arrangements and on fostering and kinship care.

Freedom of Information Act (Scotland) 2002 **FOI(S) Act 2002**

Provides a framework for accessing information held by Scottish public authorities, ensuring transparency and accountability. It grants individuals the right to request information and outlines exemptions for certain categories of information. Additionally, Scottish public authorities are required to publish information under a "publication scheme" duty.

Mental Health (Care and Treatment) (Scotland) Act 2003, as amended by the Mental Health (Scotland) Act 2015

The main pieces of mental health legislation in Scotland. There is no lower age limit and it may be used for children and young people and takes account of the welfare and interests of children and other patients.

Civil Partnership Act 2004 **CPA 2004**

Allows same-sex couples to enter into formal civil partnerships with considerable legal consequences in a wide range of matters, including inheritance, property, taxation and immigration. It has different provisions for the different parts of the UK. It does not have provisions for Scotland about parental responsibilities and rights for children. It did not enable same-sex couples to adopt in the UK, but this has been possible in England and Wales under the 2002 Act and in Scotland under the 2007 Act.

Family Law (Scotland) Act 2006 **FL(S)A 2006**

Covers a range of issues, including parental responsibilities and rights for unmarried fathers and rights for separating unmarried couples.

It amends the law relating to the domicile of persons who are under 16 years of age, and the law relating to PRRs in relation to children. The Act also confers rights in relation to property and succession.

Equality Act 2006 **EA 2006**

Established the Equality and Human Rights Commission (EHRC). It is a precursor to the Equality Act 2010.

Adoption and Children (Scotland) Act 2007 **AC(S)A 2007**

The chief source of law relating to adoption in Scotland since 28 September 2009. It broadened the range of services and duties of local authorities to provide support in both domestic and foreign adoptions. The Act aimed to improve planning for permanence and adoption for children and families and to ensure that children's interests remain central to legal and child care practice.

Protection of Vulnerable Groups (Scotland) Act 2007 **PVG(S)A 2007**

Replaced the POCSA 2003 and extended the protection system to vulnerable adults. It introduced the PVG scheme for vetting and barring. There are lists of people considered unsuitable to work with children and/or protected adults; and there are duties on organisations to refer people for possible inclusion and consequences for all people who work with children or protected adults, whether in employment or on a voluntary basis. The Disclosure (Scotland) Act 2020 (see below) will make amendments to the PVG Act and **will repeal and replace Part 5 of the Police Act 1997** as it applies in Scotland to support the modernisation of the policy design of the disclosure system.

Human Fertilisation and Embryology Act 2008 **HFEA 2008**

Substantially amended the HFEA 1990 which had established the Human Fertilisation and Embryology Authority and the regulatory structures for assisted reproduction. The law about parenthood in assisted reproduction is now in the 2008 Act which governs various aspects related to assisted reproduction, embryo research and parental rights. Additionally, the **Human Fertilisation and Embryology Act 2008 (Remedial) Order 2018** introduced changes, allowing a single person to apply for a parental order under certain conditions.

Equality Act 2010 **EA 2010**

Replaces previous anti-discrimination legislation, bringing the provisions into one Act. It restates, streamlines and harmonises equality legislation. Public authorities have responsibilities under equality legislation for ensuring that discrimination does not occur, and for promoting equality of opportunity regardless of race, sex and disability. Among the provisions it replaced were the Race Relations Act 1976, as amended by the Race Relations (Amendment) Act

2000, and the Disability Discrimination Acts 1995 and 2005. These provisions have clear relevance to all children and family services provided by local authorities.

Child protection policy must pay due regard to equality and diversity issues. Access to and delivery of child protection services should be fair, consistent, reliable, and focused on individual outcomes and enablement. Children and families should experience listening, respectful, responsive services.

These matters are eliminating conduct prohibited by the Act, advancing equality of opportunity, and fostering good relations between people who share a protected characteristic and people who do not share it. Specific duties placed on Scottish public authorities are set out in the Equality Act 2010 (Specific Duties) (Scotland) Regulations 2012 (as amended).

Public Services Reform (Scotland) Act 2010 **2010 Act**

Aimed to improve the delivery and accountability of public services in Scotland. It also grants the Scottish Ministers powers to modify the functions of certain public bodies, subject to parliamentary approval and evidence of need. The Act imposes a duty on scrutiny bodies to improve their efficiency, effectiveness and economy. Among other reforms, this replaced the Care Commission provisions in the 2001 Act.

Children's Hearings (Scotland) Act 2011 **2011 Act**

Sets out the legal basis for the care and protection of children and the duties and powers of local authorities, police officers and others to make a referral to the Principal Reporter in relation to a child. After investigation, where the Children's Reporter considers that there is sufficient evidence to require compulsory measures, the Children's Reporter must refer the child to a children's hearing.

The Act also governs the proceedings at children's hearings. It sets out emergency measures for the protection of children, including child protection and child assessment orders, emergency applications to justices of the peace and the powers of a constable to remove a child to a place of safety.

Significant changes have been made in respect of the children's hearing system under the 2024 Act (see below).

Social Care (Self-directed Support) (Scotland) Act 2013

Makes legislative provisions relating to the arranging of care and support, community care services and children's services to provide a range of choices to people for how they are provided with support. The Act enables local authorities to provide support to certain carers and makes provision about the way in which certain social care services are provided by local authorities.

Children and Young People (Scotland) Act 2014 **2014 Act**

A key part of the Scottish Government's strategy for making Scotland the best place in the world for children to grow up. There is a duty to assess the wellbeing of children and young people under the Act with reference to the eight wellbeing indicators. The commitment remains to deliver these core components of Getting it Right for Every Child (GIRFEC) within existing law. The legislation encourages preventative measures, rather than crises responses, and also establishes a new legal framework within which services (corporate parents) are to work collaboratively in support of children, young people and families.

It amends and adds to a range of provisions about children's services and **encourages Scottish Ministers and public bodies to consider children's rights, requiring them to prepare reports on what they are doing to these**. The Act introduced significant changes that would impact on every aspect of children's services and on all stages of a child's life, from birth well into adulthood.

Courts Reform (Scotland) Act 2014

Makes changes to the structure and organisation of the Scottish courts, including the establishment of the **Sheriff Appeal Court** and the simplification of civil procedure. It also amends the law of evidence, judicial review, interim orders and remit of cases.

Human Trafficking and Exploitation (Scotland) Act 2015

Clarified, strengthened and brought together the existing laws on human

trafficking. The Act makes provision about human trafficking and slavery, servitude and forced or compulsory labour, including provision about offences and sentencing, provision for victim support and provision to reduce activity related to offences. It aims to combat trafficking, protect victims and prevent further exploitation.

Education (Scotland) Act 2016

Aims to **reduce inequalities of outcomes arising out of socio-economic disadvantage** in school education. The law also gives **more rights to children aged 12 and over** who have additional support needs, allowing them to influence decision making about their education. The law applies to Scottish Ministers and local authorities who are responsible for school education.

Child Poverty (Scotland) Act 2017

Sets out targets to reduce the number of children experiencing the effects of poverty in Scotland by 2030. The Act requires Scottish Ministers to publish child poverty delivery plans at regular intervals, with annual reports to measure progress. Local authorities and health boards must also jointly publish annual reports on what they are doing to reduce child poverty in the area. The Act also established a statutory Poverty and Inequality Commission from 1 July 2019.

Limitation (Childhood Abuse) (Scotland) Act 2017

Removes the usual three-year limitation period for claims by anyone who was under the age of 18 when the abuse took place. The Act allows historic child abuse survivors to bring claims for compensation against their abusers or those responsible for them, where the abuse took place after 26 September 1964.

Data Protection Act 2018 **DPA 2018**

Sets out the rules for how personal data is used and protected by organisations, businesses or the Government. It applies to the whole of the UK and governs the keeping and release of personal data held on file about individuals. This includes social work and education information held by local authorities, but all Scottish adoption agency records are specifically exempt from the subject access provisions by regulations. Individuals are entitled to access personal data held on them and this cannot be shared with others without their consent, although there are exceptions to these rules. The system is very complicated and is monitored by the UK Information Commissioner.

Children (Equal Protection from Assault) (Scotland) Act 2019

Outlaws the use of corporal punishment on children. Where a person assaults a child under the age of 16, they cannot claim the defence of "reasonable chastisement" or "justifiable assault". By abolishing this defence, parents and carers could face prosecution for any use of physical punishment on children.

Vulnerable Witnesses (Criminal Evidence) (Scotland) Act 2019

Created a new rule for child witnesses under 18 to ensure that, where they are due to give evidence in the most serious cases, they will be allowed to have it pre-recorded in advance of the trial. This will usually be by the special measure "evidence by commissioner". The Act also makes provision for the use of special measures for the purpose of taking the evidence of children and other vulnerable witnesses in criminal or civil proceedings.

Age of Criminal Responsibility (Scotland) Act 2019

Increases the age of criminal responsibility in Scotland from **8 years to 12 years of age**. The Act introduces provisions related to the disclosure of convictions and other relevant information for children who were under 12 at the time of the offence or behaviour. The Act establishes an independent reviewer responsible for reviewing information prior to disclosure. It addresses the provision of information to victims affected by a child's behaviour. The Act deals with police investigatory powers and other powers, including the emergency place of safety, search of children under 12, and questioning of certain children.

Children (Scotland) Act 2020 **C(S)A 2020**

Will bring the law further into line with children's rights under the UNCRC; make sure children's views are heard in family court cases and children's hearings and that the best interests of children are at the centre of those cases; and give more protection to victims of domestic abuse and their children. This statute further specifies and extends the duties and rights under the Children (Scotland)

Act 1995, particularly in relation to supporting and promoting the child's participation in proceedings and in respect of recognising the importance of the rights of siblings.

Disclosure (Scotland) Act 2020

The legislative framework to modernise and improve the proportionality of the disclosure system in Scotland. It amends aspects of the PVG Act and **repealed and replaced Part 5 of the Police Act 1997**. The majority of the Act was implemented in April 2025.

Female Genital Mutilation (Protection and Guidance) (Scotland) Act 2020

Addresses the prevention of female genital mutilation (FGM). It introduces **female genital mutilation protection orders** that are designed to protect women at risk of FGM. They can be issued by the court to prevent FGM from occurring or to safeguard someone who has already undergone FGM. The Act also includes guidance related to FGM that covers both the prevention of FGM and the use of protection orders for victims. The Act makes consequential modifications to existing legislation, including amending the **Children's Hearings (Scotland) Act 2011**.

United Nations Convention on the Rights of the Child (Incorporation) (Scotland) Act 2024

Scotland incorporated the UNCRC into domestic law, endeavouring to respect, protect and fulfil children's rights. This became operational in July 2024. See above.

Children (Care and Justice) (Scotland) Act 2024 **2024 Act**

With this Act's enactment, anyone under the age of 18 (including those involved in criminality) will be referred to the Children's Reporter for any ground of referral, once this part of the forthcoming legislation is operational.

The threshold is lowered for the use of Movement Restriction Conditions which may be invoked to protect the child themselves or any possible victim. Within the hearing system, children may be detained in secure accommodation, rather than being placed in young offenders institutions, where courts dealing with their offending may have detained them.

Currently, relevant persons have wide-ranging and specific rights; whether these will apply to children over the age of 16 is uncertain, particularly taking account of the child's right to privacy.

12 Regulations, etc

Act of Sederunt (Child Care and Maintenance Rules) 1997

A set of rules for the Sheriff Court in Scotland. It consolidated various rules relating to proceedings under several Acts. These rules cover various aspects of childcare, adoption, parental responsibilities, and maintenance orders.

The following regulations amend these in various aspects of child welfare law.

Act of Sederunt (Child Care and Maintenance Rules) Amendment 2000 SSI 2000/388 (Hague Convention Adoption) 2003 SSI 2203/44; Vulnerable Witnesses (Scotland) Act 2004) 2005 SSI 2005/190; 2206/75 and 2007 SSI 2007/468; (Adoption and Children Act 2002) 2006 SSI 2006/411; Act of Sederunt (Child Care and Maintenance Rules) Amendment 2009 SSI 2009/29 and (No.2) 2009 SSI 2009/449; Act of Sederunt (Child Care and Maintenance Rules) Amendment (Human Fertilisation and Embryology Act 2008) 2010 SSI 2010/137 Act of Sederunt (Sheriff Court Adoption Rules Amendment) 2015 SSI 2015/5

Acts of Sederunt are made by the Court of Session, the supreme civil court of Scotland, to regulate the proceedings of Scottish courts and tribunals hearing civil matters. Being aware of various amendments ensures an understanding of procedures to be followed when appearing in the Court of Session.

Act of Sederunt (Rules of the Court of Session 1994 and Ordinary Court Rules 1993 Amendment) (Child Welfare Reporters) 2015 SSI2015/312; (Views of the Child) 2019 SSI 2019/223; (Attendance at Hearings) 2023 SSI2023/168 Act of Sederunt (Child Support Rules Amendment) (Miscellaneous) 2015 SSI 2015/351 Act of Sederunt (Rules of the Court of Session 1994 and Sheriff Court Rules Amendment) (Miscellaneous) 2014 SSI 2014/201; (no 2) SSI 2014/291; 2015 (no 3) SSI 2015 283; SSI 2016/102; (no 2) SSI/229; (no 3) SSI 2016/242; (no 5) 2016/384 Act of Sederunt

(Rules of the Court of Session 1994 and Child Care and Maintenance Rules 1997 Amendment (Parental Orders) 2019 SSI 2019/147 Act of Sederunt (Ordinary Cause Rules 1993 Amendment) (Case Management of Defended Family and Civil Partnership Actions) 2022 SSI 2022/289

Adoption and Children (Scotland) Act 2007 (Compulsory Supervision Order Reports in Applications for Permanence Orders) Regulations 2014

Prescribe the information that must be contained in the report prepared by the children's hearing under s.95 of the Adoption and Children (Scotland) Act 2007.

Adoption Support Services and Allowances (Scotland) Regulations 2009, SSI 2009/152 **Ad Supp Regs 2009**

Cover arrangements for adoption support services and adoption allowances.

Adoption Agencies (Scotland) Regulations 2009, SSI 2009/154, as amended by the Adoption Agencies (Scotland) Amendment Regulations 2010, SSI 2010/172, the Public Services Reform (Scotland) Act 2010 (Consequential Modifications) Order 2011, SS1 2011/211, and the Children's Hearings (Scotland) Act 2011 (Modification of Subordinate Legislation) Order 2013, SSI 2013/147

Ad Ag Regs 2009

Set out the rules for the running of adoption services (but not adoption support) by local authority and voluntary adoption agencies, including planning for children who are to be adopted.

Adoptions with a Foreign Element (Scotland) Regulations 2009, SSI 2009/182, amended by the Adoptions with a Foreign Element (Scotland) Amendment Regulations 2010, SSI 2010/173 and the Adoptions with a Foreign Element (Scotland) Amendment Regulations 2011, SSI 2011/159

Foreign Adoption Regs 2009

These are about arrangements for children involved in foreign or overseas adoptions. There are two types of foreign adoptions: where children from overseas are adopted into Scotland, usually referred to as intercountry adoptions; and where Scottish children leave the UK for adoption in overseas countries.

Adoption (Disclosure of Information and Medical Information about Natural Parents) (Scotland) Regulations 2009, SSI 2009/268 Regs 2009

Set out the rules for accessing information from adoption agency records, which are exempt from the subject access provisions of the DPA 1998. They also allow for the sharing of medical information about a child who may be adopted, even without parental permission.

Age of Criminal Responsibility (Scotland) Act 2019 (Commencement No. 1 and Transitory Provision) Regulations 2019 SSI 2019/349 (C.17); The Age of Criminal Responsibility (Scotland) Act 2019 (Commencement No. 2) Regulations 2020 SSI 2020/74 (C.7); The Age of Criminal Responsibility (Scotland) Act 2019 (Independent Review of Disclosure of Information) Regulations 2020 SSI 2020(305); The Age of Criminal Responsibility (Scotland) Act 2019 (Commencement No. 3) Regulations 2020 SSI 2020/369 (C.30); The Age of Criminal Responsibility (Scotland) Act 2019 (Register of Child Interview Rights Practitioners) Regulations 2021 SSI 2021/233; The Age of Criminal Responsibility (Scotland) Act 2019 (Supplementary Provision) (Jurisdiction) Regulations 2021 SSI2021/420; The Age of Criminal Responsibility (Scotland) Act 2019 (Places of Safety) Regulations 2021 SSI 2021/421; The Age of Criminal Responsibility (Scotland) Act 2019 (Commencement No. 4) Regulations 2021 SSI2021/449 (C.32); The Age of Criminal Responsibility (Reports on Use of Places of Safety) (Scotland) Regulations 2022 SSI 2022/293

Give specification to the legislation in relation to the Act that increases the age of criminal responsibility in Scotland to 12 years of age.

Children's Hearings (Scotland) Act 2011 (Children's Advocacy Services) Regulations 2020 SSI 2020/370

These pertain to the provision of **children's advocacy services** under s.122 of the Children's Hearings (Scotland) Act 2011. They outline the procedures and requirements related to advocacy services for children involved in hearings.

Children's Hearings (Provision of Information by Principal Reporter) (Specified Persons) (Scotland) Regulations 2020 SSI 2020/449

The Regulations specify persons who may make a request to the Principal Reporter under s.179A(3) of the **Children's Hearings (Scotland) Act 2011** for information about the action taken by the Reporter in relation to certain conduct on the part of a child. These Regulations also outline the conditions under which those persons may request and receive information from the Reporter. The specified conditions restrict the manner in which the requested information may be used by the specified persons.

Children's Hearings (Scotland) Act 2011 (Rules of Procedure in Children's Hearings) Rules 2013, SSI 2013/194; The Children's Hearings (Scotland) Act 2011 (Rules of Procedure in Children's Hearings) Amendment Rules 2015 2015/20; The Children's Hearings (Scotland) Act 2011 (Rules of Procedure in Children's Hearings) Amendment Rules 2021 2021/68; The Children's Hearings (Scotland) Act 2011 (Rules of Procedure in Children's Hearings) Amendment Rules 2022/264

Provide guidance on the procedure relating to children's hearings and pre-hearing panels under ss.177 and 195 of the Children's Hearings (Scotland) Act 2011. These rules cover various aspects related to children's hearings, including the selection of members, duties of panel members, roles of individuals attending or preparing documents, general duties of the Reporter, attendance authorisation, and more.

Children's Hearings (Scotland) Act 2011 (Safeguarders Panel) Amendment Regulations 2016 2016/61; The Children's Hearings (Scotland) Act 2011 (Safeguarders Panel) Amendment Regulations 2023 SSI 2023/66

The 2016 Regulations introduced a definition for the "Practice Standards" for Safeguarders published by the Scottish Government in 2015, which clarified the conditions for reappointment of members of the Safeguarders Panel and provided guidelines for removal of members who are not fit to serve. They also specified training requirements for members of the Safeguarders Panel. The 2023 Regulations updated these.

Regulation (EU) 2016/679 of the European Parliament and of the Council of 27 April 2016 on the protection of natural persons with regard to the processing of personal data and on the free movement of such data (United Kingdom General Data Protection Regulation) (Text with EEA relevance) the General Data Protection Regulation

GDPR

The GDPR has been incorporated into UK data protection law as the UK GDPR, which is in force alongside the Data Protection Act 2018. General principles are outlined in a Guide to the UK General Data Protection Regulation (UK GDPR) ICO and key practice considerations applicable in all child protection processes are summarised in guidance.

There are six general data principles dealing with the accuracy, relevance and purpose of the personal information and how it may be processed, collected and retained.

Children's Legal Assistance (Miscellaneous Amendments and Consequential Provisions) (Scotland) Regulations 2021 SSI 2021/368

Specify when children's legal assistance is available automatically or available on application to the Scottish Legal Aid Board and state the conditions that must be met for children's legal assistance to be made available.

Cross-Border Placements (Effect of Deprivation of Liberty Orders) (Scotland) Regulations 2022 SSI 2022/225

This instrument is made in exercise of the powers conferred by ss.190 and 195(2) of the Children's Hearings (Scotland) Act 2011. The instrument is subject to the affirmative procedure. The Regulations relate to the practice of local authorities elsewhere in the UK placing children into Scottish residential care under a Deprivation of Liberty ("DOL") order.

Human Trafficking and Exploitation (Independent Child Trafficking Guardians) (Scotland) Regulations 2023 SSI 2023/18

A set of regulations made by the Scottish Ministers in exercise of the powers conferred by s.11(7) of the **Human Trafficking and Exploitation (Scotland)**

Act 2015. The Regulations aim to address the provision of a Register for independent child trafficking guardians in Scotland.

Looked After Children (Scotland) Regulations 2009 as amended SSI 2009/210 & 290; SSI 2013/14; SSI 2014/ 310; SSI 2021/103

These set out the rules for all looked after children, fostering and arrangements between local authorities and registered fostering services. They include provisions for children's plans and medical assessments, looked after children (LAC) reviews and arrangements for fostering and kinship carers. They have been substantially amended in relation to the maximum number of children who can be cared for within a fostering setting and in promoting the importance of siblings being accommodated with or close to one another where appropriate.

Redress for Survivors (Historical Child Abuse in Care) (Scotland) Regulations 2021 (Reimbursement of Costs and Expenses) SSI 2021/312; (Payment of Legal Fees) SSI 2021/313; (Exceptions to Eligibility) SSI 2021/413; (Form and Content of Waiver etc.) SSI 2021/414; (Payments Materially Affected by Error) SSI 2021/479; The Redress for Survivors (Historical Child Abuse in Care) (Reconsideration and Review of Determinations (Scotland) Regulations 2022 SSI 2022/44

Scotland's Adoption Register Regulations 2016 SSI 2016/154

These were created to **set out the key requirements for supplying, retaining and disclosing information**. All adoption agencies in Scotland use Scotland's Adoption Register to refer both children and adopters within three months of approval.

Scottish Child Payment Regulations 2020 and the Disability Assistance for Children and Young People (Scotland) Regulations 2021 (Miscellaneous Amendments) Regulations 2022 SS1 2021/73; SSI 2021/174; 2021/416; 2022/41; 2023/346

Regulations relating to social security benefits in Scotland.

The Secure Accommodation (Scotland) Regulations 2013 SSI 2013/205; The Children's Hearings (Scotland) Act 2011 (Implementation of Secure

Accommodation Authorisation) (Scotland) Regulations 2013 SSI 2013/212; The Secure Accommodation (Scotland) Amendment Regulations 2015 SSI 2015/20; 2016 SSI 2016/45 2016 no.45 Scottish Statutory Instruments

13 Court rules

NB These are all available on the Scottish Courts website.

Act of Sederunt (Sheriff Court Ordinary Cause Rules) 1993 (as amended)

These are for a wide range of sheriff court cases called Ordinary Causes. They include applications in family cases under the 1995 Act, such as residence and contact orders, and divorce proceedings. These rules govern the preparation of court reports which may be ordered in these cases.

Act of Sederunt (Child Care and Maintenance Rules) 1997 AS 1997

A set of rules for the Sheriff Court in Scotland. It consolidated various rules relating to proceedings under several Acts. These rules cover various aspects of childcare, adoption, parental responsibilities, and maintenance orders.

The following Regulations amend these:

Act of Sederunt (Child Care and Maintenance Rules) Amendment 2000 SSI 2000/388; Act of Sederunt (Hague Convention Adoption) 2003 SSI 2003/44; Act of Sederunt (Vulnerable Witnesses (Scotland) Act 2004) 2005 SSI 2005/190; 2206/75 and 2007 SSI 2007/468; Act of Sederunt (Child Care and Maintenance Rules 1997) (Amendment) (Adoption and Children Act 2002) 2006 2006 SSI 2006/411; Act of Sederunt (Child Care and Maintenance Rules) Amendment 2009 SSI 2009/29 (No.2) 2009 SSI 2009/449; Act of Sederunt (Child Care and Maintenance Rules) Amendment (Human Fertilisation and Embryology Act 2008) 2010 SSI 2010/137; Act of Sederunt (Rules and the Court of Session 1994 and Child Care and Maintenance Rules 1997 Amendment) (Parental Orders) 2019 SSI 2019/147 2019 No. 147 Scottish Statutory Instruments

Schedule to the Act of Sederunt (Sheriff Court Rules Amendment) (Adoption and Children (Scotland) Act 2007) 2009, SSI 2009/284, as amended Sheriff Court Adoption Rules 2009 amended by Act of Sederunt (Sheriff Court

Adoption Rules Amendment) 2015 SSI 2015/5

The court rules for applications in the Sheriff Court under the 2007 Act, for adoption, permanence orders and related matters.

Act of Sederunt (Summary Applications, Statutory Applications and Appeals etc. Rules 1999 and Sheriff Appeal Court Rules Amendment) (Age of Criminal Responsibility (Scotland) Act 2019) 2021 SSI2021/452

Act of Sederunt (Rules of the Court of Session 1994 and Ordinary Court Rules 1993: Act of Sederunt (Rules of the Court of Session) 1994 (as amended) **RCS**

Court rules for Court of Session cases, with forms. They cover all cases, including *Family Actions* (Chapter 49), and *Adoption* (Chapter 67).

Being aware of various amendments ensures an understanding of procedures to be followed when appearing in the Court of Session.

They have been subject to a number of amendments in recent years:

Amendment (Child Welfare Reporters) 2015 SSI2015/312; (Views of the Child) 2019 SSI 2019/223; (Attendance at Hearings) 2023 SSI2023/168 Act of Sederunt (Child Support Rules Amendment) (Miscellaneous) 2015 SSI 2015/351; Act of Sederunt (Rules of the Court of Session 1994 and Sheriff Court Rules Amendment) (Miscellaneous) 2014 SSI 2014/201; (no 2) SSI 2014/291; 2015 (no 3) SSI 2015 283; SSI 2016/102; (no 2) SSI/229; (no 3) SSI 2016/242; (no 5) 2016/384

Act of Sederunt (Rules of the Court of Session 1994 and Child Care and Maintenance Rules 1997 Amendment (Parental Orders) 2019 SSI 2019/147 Act of Sederunt (Ordinary Cause Rules 1993 Amendment) (Case Management of Defended Family and Civil Partnership Actions) 2022 SSI 2022/289

14 Guidance

There is a range of guidance relevant to child care law. It is available on the Scottish Government website – see Further Reading. The principal guidance is:

Scotland's Children: The Children (Scotland) Act 1995, Regulations and Guidance, Volume 1: Support and protection for children and their families

1995 Act Guidance

Guidance on the Looked After Children (Scotland) Regulations 2009 and the Adoption and Children (Scotland) Act 2007 (issued 10 March 2011)[2]

2007 Act Guidance

Private Fostering in Scotland: Practice guidance for local authority children's services (issued 29 November 2013)[3]

Private Fostering Guidance

National Guidance for Child Protection in Scotland 2021 (updated 2023)[4]

This non-statutory guidance describes responsibilities and expectations for all involved in protecting children in Scotland. It outlines how statutory and non-government agencies should work together with parents, families and communities to prevent harm and protect children from abuse and neglect.

Social Care (Self-directed Support) (Scotland) Act 2013: Statutory guidance 2014 (updated 2022)[5]

Staying Together and Connected: Getting it right for sisters and brothers: national practice guidance (2021)[6]

There have been several guidances issued by the Scottish Government in relation to the Children and Young People (Scotland) Act 2014:

2 https://www.gov.scot/publications/guidance-looked-children-scotland-regulations-2009-adoption-children-scotland-act-2007/

3 https://www.gov.scot/binaries/content/documents/govscot/publications/advice-and-guidance/2013/11/private-fostering-scotland-practice-guidance-local-authority-childrens-services/documents/00439291-pdf/00439291-pdf/govscot%3Adocument/00439291.pdf

4 https://www.gov.scot/publications/national-guidance-child-protection-scotland-2021-updated-2023/documents/

5 https://www.gov.scot/publications/statutory-guidance-accompany-social-care-self-directed-support-scotland-act-2013-2/

6 https://www.gov.scot/publications/staying-together-connected-getting-right-sisters-brothers-national-practice-guidance/

Children And Young People (Scotland) Act 2014: Statutory guidance on Part 3: Children's services planning (second edition 2020)[7]

Children And Young People (Scotland) Act 2014: Part 6: Early learning and childcare[8]

Children And Young People (Scotland) Act 2014: Statutory guidance on Part 9 (Corporate Parenting)[9]

Children and Young People (Scotland) Act 2014: Guidance on Part 10 (Aftercare)[10]

Children and Young People (Scotland) Act: 2014: Guidance on Part 11 (Continuing Care)[11]

Children And Young People (Scotland) Act 2014: National guidance on Part 12: Services in relation to children at risk of becoming looked after, etc[12]

Children and Young People (Scotland) Act 2014 (Support for Kinship Care) Guidance on Part 13 and The Kinship Care Assistance (Scotland) Order 2016 (updated guidance 2024)[13]

15 Standards

7 https://www.gov.scot/publications/children-young-people-scotland-act-2014-statutory-guidance-part-3-childrens-services-planning-second-edition-2020/

8 https://www.gov.scot/binaries/content/documents/govscot/publications/advice-and-guidance/2014/08/early-learning-childcare-statutory-guidance/documents/00457025-pdf/00457025-pdf/govscot%3Adocument/00457025.pdf

9 https://www.gov.scot/publications/statutory-guidance-part-9-corporate-parenting-children-young-people-scotland/

10 https://www.gov.scot/publications/guidance-part-10-aftercare-children-young-people-scotland-act-2014/

11 https://www.gov.scot/publications/guidance-part-11-continuing-care-children-young-people-scotland-act/documents/

12 https://www.gov.scot/publications/children-young-people-scotland-act-2014-national-guidance-part-12/pages/3/

13 https://www.gov.scot/publications/part-13-children-young-people-scotland-act-2014-support-kinship-care-kinship-care-assistance-scotland-order-2016-updated-guidance-2024/

National Care Standards: Adoption agencies (revised March 2005)[14]

National Care Standards: Foster care and family placement services (2011)[15]

Health and Social Care Standards: My support, my life (2017)[16]

16 Other abbreviations

Legislation

1937 Act	Children and Young Persons (Scotland) Act 1937
1968 Act	Social Work (Scotland) Act 1968
1975 Act	Children Act 1975
1985 Act	Family Law (Scotland) Act 1985
1986 Act	Law Reform (Parent and Child) (Scotland) Act 1986
FLA 1986	Family Law Act 1986
1989 Act	Children Act 1989
CSA 1991	Child Support Act 1991
CP(S)A 1995	Criminal Procedure (Scotland) Act 1995
ASBA 2004	Antisocial Behaviour etc (Scotland) Act 2004
FM Act 2011	Forced Marriage etc (Protection and Jurisdiction) (Scotland) Act 2011

14 https://www.gov.scot/publications/national-care-standards-adoption-agencies-revised-march-2005/pages/1/

15 https://www.gov.scot/publications/national-care-standards-foster-care-family-placement-services/

16 https://www.gov.scot/publications/health-social-care-standards-support-life/

2

General principles and children's rights and capacity

This chapter deals with general themes and principles in the law of Scotland relating to children, some of which are in legislation from 1995 onwards (the 1995, 2007, 2011, 2014, 2020 and 2024 Acts).

1 Definition of "child"

There is no single definition of "child" in the law of Scotland. Whether a young person is a child or not will depend on particular legislation and/or circumstances.

However, as a rule of thumb, 16-year-olds in Scotland may do most things legally except buy alcohol (age 18) or drive (age 17). In private disputes about children between parents and other carers, the law usually regulates the position only up to the age of 16, although parents are obliged to pay maintenance for their children beyond that time and until they finish all education. Where a child is looked after by the local authority, continuing care can last up to the child's 21st birthday and there is provision for after-care beyond up to their 26th birthday.

The UNCRC defines a child as any person under the age of 18 'unless under the law applicable to the child, majority is attained earlier'.[17] With the incorporation of the UNCRC,[18] it will be interesting to learn how this will be interpretated moving forward in Scots law pertaining to children.

17 Layout 1 (unicef.org.uk) Article 1

18 United Nations Convention on the Rights of the Child (Incorporation) (Scotland) Act (legislation.gov.uk)

2 Principles to be applied

The 1995 Act introduced or re-stated principles that apply to most decisions in the areas of law it covered, and these were further reflected in subsequent legislation. The fundamental considerations have prevailed but the 2020 Act significantly reinforced the rights of children involved in legal processes, with the effect that decisions be made with them and not to them.

These "overarching principles" are stated below.

Those areas included private law, local authority duties, child protection measures, the children's hearing system, and adoption. Some of the provisions are covered by the 1995 Act, but the principles (or "considerations") have been carried forward into these subsequent Acts. The principles are set out below.

2.1 Child's welfare to be paramount consideration or concern

This was not a completely new test in all types of cases in the 1995 Act, but is the test that applies in court decisions, children's hearings' decisions and local authority and adoption agency decisions about welfare.

In private law cases this has been the test since 1986. Under the 2007 Act, the test in adoption is that the child's welfare throughout the child's life shall be of paramount consideration. In applications for permanence orders with authority to adopt, the courts have also applied this principle. In all other cases, including applications for permanence orders, the test is the child's welfare throughout childhood. In addition to this duty, the 2014 Act contains a "wellbeing" duty on local authorities in providing services to children in need, looked after children and children receiving continuing care.

ss.11(7)(a) and (7A)–(7E) and 17(1)(a) 1995 Act; ss.14(3) and 84(4) 2007 Act; s.25 2011 Act; ss.95 and 96 2014 Act; Looked After Regs 2009; case law in relation to POAs

2.2 Minimum necessary intervention

This principle is sometimes called the "no order" principle. It states that no court order or children's hearing order shall be made unless the court/hearing thinks that making an order is better for the child than not making it. This does not mean that making an order is a "last resort". It means that the court or hearing must be certain that an order is necessary for the child's welfare, and that the order it is making is the best one and proportionate. If the child's welfare can be secured as a paramount consideration without an order or with less of an order, that is what should be done. Adoption agencies have a similar duty when they are making any decisions relating to the adoption of a child: they must consider alternatives.

s.11(7)(a) 1995 Act; ss.14(6) and (7), s.28(2) and s.84(3) 2007 Act; ss.28 and 29 2011 Act

2.3 Consideration of the child's views

Courts, children's hearings, local authorities and adoption agencies all have a duty to allow children to express their views about their situations, and to take account of these views in their decisions. While this had been good practice in many areas, the 1995 Act formally introduced it as a duty in these situations, and subsequent legislation has reiterated and reinforced this duty. There is no lower age limit and the previous presumption of maturity being reached when the child became 12 has been removed. It is necessary *in all cases* to find out:

- if children have views;
- whether they wish to express them; and if so,
- to take account of the views.

The Children (Scotland) Act 2020 made provisions to ensure that the child's views are heard and to enable the child's participation in proceedings where decisions are being made about them. The child is to be presumed to be capable of forming a view unless the contrary is shown.

2.4 Responsibility of adults and exceptions

Adults should:

> *...seek to make reasonable arrangements for the child to express the child's views in a manner that the child has indicated the child prefers, and have regard to any views expressed by the child, taking into account the child's age and maturity.*

The court or adoption agency is not required to comply, if satisfied that the child is not capable of forming a view or the child's whereabouts are unknown.

2.5 Child's views in reports

Consideration should be given to seeking and communicating the child's views in profiling the child and this should be reviewed throughout the process. This places an obligation on report writers to ensure that information they are providing to decision-makers and parties about the child are accurate and, importantly, up to date. Professionals are obliged to gain and apply the child's views to inform their decision-making and the child should not need to adapt how and to whom they communicate to fit in with adults.

2.6 Child's views in children's hearings

There existed a duty on the chairing member in a children's hearing to make reasonable arrangements to enable the child to express their views in their preferred manner. This right has been extended in terms of the 2020 Act.

A children's advocate shall be available to a child to support them in expressing their views at the children's hearing. It is expected that digital developments in the future will offer greater flexibility for the ways in which children can give their views.

Children's hearings and sheriffs in court procedures resulting from children's hearings may appoint a Safeguarder for the child who will include in their report the views of the child.

2.7 Child's views in court

In referrals to court, the sheriff may order such procedural steps to be taken as they consider appropriate to ascertain the views of the child. The court is required to appoint a curator ad litem in every case and the child could, if the curator considers it appropriate, speak directly to the sheriff.

Where courts are making decisions about a child in family matters under the Children (Scotland) Act 1995, they will have to make sure that their decision is explained to the child in a way that the child can understand. Either the sheriff will explain it face to face, electronically or by letter, or the court can ask a Child Welfare Reporter to explain the decision to the child.

In 2017, a sheriff wrote to two children to explain her decision in a contact case between their parents. She did so at the suggestion of a clinical psychologist and using age-appropriate language for the children to understand her reasoning.[19]

2.8 *Non conflation of views being sought and decision being made*

It is important that when a child expresses their view, they understand that this will be listened to and taken into account but that the decision of the court may be different from what the child wants.

3 Child's views and the UNCRC

The new provisions to enable the child's expression of their views and participation in proceedings is consistent with Article 12 of the UNCRC, which requires state parties to:

> *Guarantee to all children capable of forming their own views, the right to express their views freely in all matters affecting them;*
>
> *Ensure that children's views be given due weight in accordance with their age and maturity;*
>
> *Provide children with the opportunity to be heard in judicial and*

19 Letter-to-the-children.pdf (msmlaw.co.uk)

administrative proceedings, either directly or indirectly.

4 Child's views and The Promise

The Promise (p.12) states that:

> *Children must be listened to and meaningfully and appropriately involved in decision-making about their care, with all those involved properly listening and responding to what they want and need. There must be a compassionate and caring decision-making culture focused on children and those they trust.*[20]

5 Child's consent in permanence proceedings

In relation to permanence decisions, an adoption order or permanence order cannot be made if a child aged 12 years or over does not give consent and is considered to have capacity to do so.

ss.6(1), 11(7)(b) and (10), s.17(3) and (4) and s.25(5) 1995 Act; ss.14(4)(b) and (8), 84(5)(a), (b)(i) and (6) 2007 Act; s.27 2011 Act; Looked After Children Regs 2009

6 Corporate parents

Corporate parenting is about certain organisations listening to the needs, fears and wishes of children and young people, and being proactive and determined in their collective efforts to meet them.

Children and Young People (Scotland) Act 2014: Statutory guidance on Part 9: Corporate parenting

7 Criminal, civil and medical, including capacity of children and young people

20 https://www.carereview.scot/wp-content/uploads/2020/02/The-Promise.pdf, p.12

7.1 Criminal capacity of children and young people

The age of criminal capacity in Scotland is 12, below which age a child is deemed to lack the capacity to commit a crime.

s.1 Age of Criminal Responsibility (Scotland) Act 2019

Since 1933, children as young as 8 could be held responsible for criminal acts – the lowest age in Europe and one of the lowest in the world. Since 28 March 2011, a child aged under 12 could not be prosecuted in the adult criminal courts, following implementation of s.52 of the Criminal Justice and Licensing (Scotland) Act 2010. However, a child aged between 8 and 12 could still be referred to a children's hearing on offence grounds, which would mean that they would then have a criminal record. This stigmatisation was contrary to a child's best interests and in May 2019 the Scottish Parliament voted unanimously to change this under the 2019 Act. This came fully into force in December 2021.

The UN Committee on the Rights of the Child stated that age 12 is the 'absolute minimum'; anything lower is not considered 'internationally acceptable' and that it should be raised to 14 'immediately'. At the time, the Scottish Government said that it had set up an advisory group to review the new provisions and it would consider whether the age should be raised further; there has been no further change.

7.2 Civil capacity

The legal age of capacity in Scotland is 16. This is a legal absolute in reference to a whole range of rights, but there are some surprising anomalies in terms of what children may and may not do.

The most striking of these specific exceptions are the rights to instruct a solicitor and to consent to medical, dental or surgical treatment.

ss.1 and 2, particularly s.2(4), (4A) and (4B) 1991 Act

7.3 Legal capacity and medical intervention for children under the age of 16

From a medical perspective, consent to any dental, surgical or medical procedure or practice must come from the young person under the age of 16 if, in the opinion of the qualified medical practitioner, the child is capable of understanding the nature and possible consequences of the proposed examination or procedure.

Children who are assessed as having capacity to consent can withhold their consent to any part of the medical examination, for example, the taking of blood, or a video recording. Consent must be documented within medical notes and must reflect which parts of the process have been consented to and by whom. This includes consent to forensic medical examination.

Parental consent is not needed in these circumstances and cannot override the child's consent or refusal, but it is good practice to work with the family as a whole, if possible. Nothing in the 2011 Act interferes with the child's capacity under the 1991 Act. This means that even where a children's hearing has issued a medical assessment order or placed a measure on another order in terms of medical, dental or surgical treatment, the child, if they refuse to consent, cannot be subjected to any such procedure.

s.2(4) 1991 Act; s.186 2011 Act

In order to ensure that children and their families give properly informed consent to medical examinations, it is the role of the examining doctor, assisted if necessary by a social worker or police officer, to provide information about all aspects of the procedure and how the results may be used; and to ensure informed consent has been obtained.

If the child is not capable of consenting themselves, consent will need to be sought from a person with parental responsibility. Children not considered to be capable of making their own decisions cannot either give or withhold consent. Those with parental responsibility need to make the decision on their behalf.

Parental responsibility to provide guidance lasts until a child reaches the age of 18, although all the other responsibilities and rights only last until the child is 16. This is the same for a child who may remain subject to a permanence order granted under the Adoption and Children (Scotland) Act 2007 or a compulsory supervision order issued under the Children's Hearings (Scotland) Act 2011.

s.1 1995 Act

8 Legal capacity and medical intervention for children aged 16 and 17

Therefore, 16- and 17-year-olds can consent to medical treatment or intervention without practitioners being concerned about assessing the young person's capacity solely due to their age or in seeking parental consent. Doctors have a duty of confidentiality to 16- and 17-year-olds and should not disclose information to parents without the patient's consent.

8.1 Specific issues order

Where the parent with parental responsibilities and rights (PRRs) is withholding their consent to treatment or procedure, a specific issues order may be sought from the court. The court will consider the application, taking account of the overarching principles of minimum intervention, considering the views of the child and will make a decision which is in the best interests of the child. The views of those with PRRs will be taken into account and evidence will be provided to assist the court in coming to a decision.

A local authority cannot make an application to the court for a specific issues order.

s.11 1995 Act

Where the local authority believes that a medical examination is required to find out whether concerns about a child's safety or welfare are justified, and parents refuse consent, the local authority may apply to a sheriff for a child assessment order, or a child protection order with a condition of medical examination. This is still subject to the child's consent.

8.2 Incapacity to consent for young people over the age of 16

If a young person over the age of 16 lacks the capacity to consent, they should be treated as an adult who lacks capacity.

In such circumstances, medical practitioners may authorise treatment to be given to safeguard or promote the physical or mental health of an adult who is unable to provide consent themselves. This can be carried out on the completion of a medical certificate of Incapacity.

8.3 Adults with Incapacity (Scotland) Act 2000, particularly s.47

The certificate can only last for a maximum of one year or, in some exceptional circumstances/conditions, up to three years. The benefit to the patient should be held at the forefront of decision-making – the wishes of the patient should be considered; there should be consultation with relevant others, including nearest relatives, and each treatment must be considered individually.

The authority to provide medical treatment under a section 47 certificate does not apply where an application has been made to the sheriff for an intervention or guardianship order with powers that cover the medical treatment in question. Until the application has been determined, medical treatment under section 47 cannot be given unless it is authorised by any other enactment or rule of law for the preservation of the life of the adult or the prevention of serious deterioration in their medical condition.

A welfare guardian or intervener is appointed by the sheriff for a person who lacks capacity to make decisions on behalf of an adult lacking capacity. The guardian or intervener will have been granted powers within the guardianship or intervention order that allow them to look after the adult's affairs. These can be financial and/or related to the personal welfare of the adult, including medical matters.

There are provisions within the Act in the event of disagreement between the medical practitioner and the Welfare Guardian.

8.4 A person with care or control of a child under the age of 16 but without PRRs

This would include foster carers and for those who have care or control of the child, it is their responsibility to do what is reasonable in all the circumstances to safeguard the child's health, development and welfare. In fulfilling their responsibility under this section, the person may, in particular, even though they do not have the parental right, give consent to any surgical, medical or dental treatment or procedure where:

- the child is not able to give such consent on their own behalf; and
- it is not within the knowledge of the person that a parent of the child would refuse to give the consent in question.

s.5 1995 Act

9 Mental health legislation review

The mental health legislation review recognises the importance of human rights. There is currently a review of various aspects of mental health and incapacity legislation use in Scotland.[21]

21 https://www.gov.scot/publications/mental-health-strategy-2017-2027/

3

Scottish courts and the criminal system

This chapter outlines briefly the Scottish court structure and explains some points about the Scottish criminal system in general. Different decisions are made in different courts. Who makes a decision, and the procedure used, depends on which court is dealing with a case.

1 Court reforms

The civil justice system was reformed with the purpose of addressing perceived inefficiencies and to achieve accessibility and cost efficiency. It became fully operational in 2016.

Courts Reform (Scotland) Act 2014

Provisions were introduced with the aim of making the expenses in civil litigation more predictable and affordable, and thus improve access to justice. Provisions were also made for a group proceedings procedure.

Civil Litigation (Expenses and Group Proceedings) (Scotland) Act 2018

2 The court system

The Scottish court system is reasonably straightforward. There are four courts that deal with civil matters, excluding the Scottish Land Court:

- Sheriff courts
- Sheriff Appeal Court (civil)

- Court of Session
- Supreme Court

And there are four courts that deal with criminal matters:

- Justice of the Peace Courts, including the Stipendiary Magistrate Court in Glasgow
- Sheriff courts
- Sheriff Appeal Court
- High Court of Justiciary

In addition, however, some criminal matters may be appealed from the High Court to the Supreme Court, in certain circumstances.

3 Human rights

All courts are public authorities under the HRA 1998, so all court decisions must take account of the ECHR.

HRA 1998

4 Civil courts

4.1 Sheriff courts

Sheriff courts operate in civil, children's hearing and criminal cases and deal with the widest variety of matters. Actions with a value of up to and including £100,000 fall within the exclusive competence of the sheriff courts. Furthermore, actions pertaining to personal injury valued up to and including £100,000 may either be heard in a litigant's local sheriff court or in the national personal injury court in Edinburgh.

Scotland is divided into six Sheriffdoms, each of which has a Sheriff Principal.

There are 39 sheriff courts, each of which has a court where a sheriff sits regularly. Sheriffs are either permanent or part-time judges. Both of these have to be legally qualified and have had a number of years' experience. Temporary sheriffs may also be appointed when there is a shortage of other sheriffs.

Summary sheriffs may also sit in the sheriff courts and their jurisdiction is limited to hearing cases where the amount sought is less than £5,000. They have authority to hear cases that involve adoption, children's hearings, warrants and interim orders, domestic abuse, diligence proceedings, extension of time to pay debts and simple procedure.

4.2 Sheriff Appeal Court (Civil)

The Sheriff Appeal Court replaced the process of sheriff court decisions being heard by the Sheriff Principal of that jurisdiction. It prevents direct appeals of sheriffs' decisions to the Court of Session, thus ensuring that cases are dealt with appropriately within the sheriff court system. It has exclusive jurisdiction for all appeals in civil cases at first instance in the sheriff courts and Sheriff Personal Injury Court. The court will appoint the appeal to the procedure that it considers proportionate for the disposal of the appeal – either under **Chapter 7 or Chapter 8 procedure**.

An appeal under **Chapter 7 procedure** will usually take place within Parliament House, Edinburgh, before a bench of three Appeal Sheriffs.

An appeal under **Chapter 8 procedure** will take place before one Appeal Sheriff within the sheriffdom where the original action took place and usually within the same sheriff court building. It may also be heard by written submissions.

The final judgement of the Sheriff Appeal Court may be appealed to the Court of Session once permission is granted by the Sheriff Appeal Court, or, if refused, by the Court of Session.

4.3 Court of Session

The Court of Session is the supreme civil court, which sits exclusively in

Parliament House in Edinburgh. It is a court of first instance and a court of appeal. The judges are legally qualified and also sit in the High Court of Justiciary. They may be permanent or temporary appointments.

The senior judge in Scotland and the head of the Scottish legal system is the Lord President of the Court of Session. They are also the Lord Justice General in criminal cases.

Where a case is started in the Court of Session, it is heard by a single judge in the "Outer House". If the court is sitting as an appeal court, a group of three or more judges sits to hear the case in the "Inner House". This deals with appeals from sheriffs and Civil Appeal Courts and the Outer House.

4.4 Appeals

The decision of the Inner House can be appealed to the Supreme Court, but only where permission has been granted by the Court of Session itself, or where permission has been refused, from the Supreme Court.

There is an appeal in some but not all civil matters from the Inner House of the Court of Session to the Supreme Court. Adoption, permanence order and permanence order with authority to adopt appeals and appeals in private law disputes about children may go to the Supreme Court. The Supreme Court does not directly hear appeals in relation to decisions made by individual children's hearings from Scotland; however, it has ruled on the compatibility of the system with human rights, including the rights of siblings to participate in the process.

4.5 Supreme Court

In the Supreme Court, the judges are called Supreme Court Justices (SCJs). Usually, five of them hear a case and if it is a Scottish appeal, two of those judges will, by convention, be Scottish. At any one time, there are always two Scottish Justices.

Justices are no longer automatically made Life Peers, although some individuals may coincidentally be Peers. The Lord Chancellor is the head of the legal system for England and Wales, but not of the Scottish legal system.

5 The Scottish criminal system

Prosecution in Scotland is carried out by an independent prosecution service. This is headed by the Crown Office and represented locally by procurators fiscal (PFs). The organisation is called the Crown Office and Procurator Fiscal Service (COPFS).

5.1 Decisions to prosecute

Decisions to prosecute are made on the basis of the following questions:

- Is there sufficient evidence? *and*
- Is it in the public interest to prosecute?

5.2

The prosecution decides what offence a person will be charged with, and which court will deal with the matter. A case is either **summary**, when it is dealt with by a judge alone; or **solemn**, when it is dealt with by a judge and jury. There is no right to jury trial in Scotland.

5.3 Reporting and referral of children

In Scotland, the age of criminal capacity is 12, but up until the age of 18, children and young people will not be prosecuted in the adult criminal courts. Instead, they are referred by the police to the Children's Reporter, who decides whether to take the case to a children's hearing.

5.4 Joint Reporting to the Reporter and Procurator Fiscal

By and large, the police report children under 18 to the Reporter alone. They are also required to report certain cases jointly to the Procurator Fiscal (PF), where the offence is more serious. If a case is jointly reported, the PF makes the ultimate decision about whether the child is dealt with in the adult system even if they are still subject to a compulsory supervision order in the hearings system.

5.5

In deciding whether to prosecute a child who has been jointly reported, the Crown Office and Procurator Fiscal Service (COPFS) will liaise with the Children's Reporter (as per their joint agreement) and will take into account a number of factors, including, for example, sufficiency of evidence, the offending history of the accused, the severity of the offence and the public interest.

This is the protocol for when a child is jointly reported to the PF and the Children's Reporter, the presumption being that the child will be referred to the Reporter if under the age of 18.

6 Legislative changes

Legislation enacted in 2024 makes a number of significant changes in how children and young people are treated and supported.

6.1

It changes the definition of "child" in the children's hearings system to someone under the age of 18, regardless of whether they are subject to a compulsory supervision order. This means that a young person under the age of 18 who commits an offence will be referred to the Children's Reporter; previously it was only those under the age of 16 who were not already subject to a compulsory supervision order who could be referred to the Children's Reporter.

6.2

There are also changes in where a child should be held awaiting the decision or trial and if prosecuted, no person under the age of 18 will be sent to a young offenders institute, instead, where appropriate, being remitted to a secure unit.

ss.1, 21 and 22 2024 Act

6.3 Parenting orders and movement restriction orders

The ASBA 2004 introduced various provisions affecting young people under 16. These involve the courts in a civil and criminal capacity, and the hearings system.

ASBA 2004

7 Criminal courts

7.1 Justice of the Peace Court

These courts deal only with minor criminal matters. Cases are heard by one or more lay, unqualified justices, sitting with a legally qualified clerk. In Glasgow, the JP Court may be presided over by a stipendiary magistrate, who is legally qualified and sits on their own. As in all criminal courts, cases come to Justice of the Peace Courts on the basis of decisions by the prosecution service.

7.2 Sheriff courts

Sheriff courts deal with the bulk of criminal cases in Scotland. They deal both with summary matters (lesser crimes) where a sheriff sits and hears the case on their own; and more serious cases (solemn matters), which are heard by a sheriff sitting with a jury. Again, decisions to take cases to the sheriff court, and whether with or without a jury, are made by the prosecution service.

7.3 Sheriff Appeal Court

The Sheriff Appeal Court is a national court that hears all appeals from summary criminal proceedings[22] in the sheriff courts and justice of the peace courts and

22 https://en.wikipedia.org/wiki/Summary_offence

appeals relating to bail[23] decisions, in both summary and solemn proceedings.[24] Bail hearings are presided over by a single appeal sheriff, while in other appeals the bench normally comprises two or three appeal sheriffs, with no jury in either case. The court sits in Edinburgh.

Decisions of this court may be appealed to the High Court of Justiciary, but only where permission is granted either by the Sheriff Appeal Court or High Court.

7.4 The High Court of Justiciary

This court deals with serious criminal trials as a court of first instance and also a court of appeal. Where sitting as a court of first instance hearing a criminal trial, this is done by one judge sitting with a jury of 15. The court goes on circuit round the country, with permanent bases in Edinburgh, Glasgow or Aberdeen. It sits periodically in Dumbarton, Lanark, Livingston, Paisley and Stirling.

As a court of appeal, it sits only in Edinburgh and hears appeals from the lower courts and from the High Court itself when it sits as a court of first instance. Two judges[25] sit to hear an appeal against sentence, and three judges sit to hear an appeal against conviction.

The judges are the same as those in the Court of Session.

7.5 Appeals

The High Court of Justiciary is the final court of appeal in Scotland for many criminal matters relating to the facts of convictions, or sentencing. However, appeals to the Supreme Court are possible in relation to alleged breaches of the correct procedures in criminal cases and issues of incompatibility with the ECHR. However, it remains the case that the Supreme Court may not review the decisions of the High Court simply on matters of Scots criminal law.

23 https://en.wikipedia.org/wiki/Bail
24 https://en.wikipedia.org/wiki/Solemn_proceedings
25 https://en.wikipedia.org/wiki/Senator_of_the_College_of_Justice

4

Parentage and parental responsibilities and rights

The law will regulate some family relationships, particularly where there is a dispute between the parents or between the parents and the State, involving a child. There are circumstances in which the State will intervene in the parent–child relationship, normally where the minimum standards of parenting have not been met. There is a distinction between private and public law.

Parental responsibilities and rights (PRRs) is the framework the law sets out for the care and control of children, and how parents and those with PRRs carry out their parenting role.

This chapter deals with the parentage of children and parental responsibilities and rights in relation to them. It covers who are parents, who has responsibilities and rights, who can get them and how, together with how the court deals with disputes in this area.

1 Parental responsibilities and rights

The 1995 Act introduced the terminology of PRRs, instead of just parental rights. Traditionally, Scots law treated children as the possession of their parents but the 1995 Act moved away from this, towards treating children as people who have their own rights as well.

1.1

Parental responsibilities are in place to support parents in discharging rights.

The responsibilities are:

- to safeguard and protect the child's welfare;
- to provide guidance;
- to maintain contact if not living with the child; and
- to act as the child's legal representative if need be.

The rights are:

- to have the child living with them;
- to control, direct or guide the child;
- to maintain contact if not living with the child; and
- to act as the child's legal representative if need be.

ss.1 and 2 1995 Act

1.2

These rights can be exercised individually by any person having them, without having to obtain the consent of anyone else who also has them. The only exception is that the child cannot be removed from the UK without the consent of every person who has the responsibilities and rights of residence and/or contact *and* is exercising them.

ss.2(2), (3) and (6) 1995 Act

2 Duty to maintain (provide financial support)

The child's mother and father, whether married/in a civil partnership or not, are both obliged to maintain a child even if they do not have any responsibilities and rights, unless the child has been adopted or made the subject of an order under the HFEA 2008. This is dealt with by the 1986 Act, not the 1995 Act.

s.1 1986 Act; s.40 2007 Act; HFEA 2008, s.54 HFEA 2008

3 Child support on divorce or separation

When parents separate or are otherwise disputing maintenance, courts are not usually involved. The Child Support Act 1991 established the Child Support Agency and the Child Support Scheme 1993. There is considerable subsequent legislation, which has led to the Child Support Scheme 2003 and, from December 2012, the 2012 Child Maintenance Scheme. This is a complex area of practice and advice in individual cases should be sought from specialists.

Child Support Acts 1991 and 1995, Child Support, Pensions and Social Security Act 2000 and Child Maintenance and Other Payments Act 2008

4 Parentage: legal mother and father

The rules of parentage are about who is considered to be the legal mother or father of a child. These rules do *not* say who has responsibilities and rights for a child – that is covered below. The law records and determines who is considered to be the legal child of an adult. This will be recorded on the birth certificate, but this may subsequently be changed with the removal of PRRs or by Declarators of Paternity or non-paternity.

5 Automatic responsibilities and rights (PRRs): mother

The common, non-statutory law did not deal with who was/is the legal mother of a child, because it is only recently that there was any possibility that the gestational mother could be a different person from the genetic mother. In most cases, there is no physical difference, but the law has a separate set of rules in relation to assisted reproduction.

The legal genetic mother automatically has PRRs, unless and until these are taken away from her by some form of court process such as adoption or a parental order under the HFEA 2008.

s.3 1995 Act

6 Automatic responsibilities and rights (PRRs): father

In unassisted conception, parenthood follows biology and the genetic connection so the genetic father may be deemed to be the legal father. However, there may be uncertainty about who is the genetic father (without DNA testing).

Unlike the position of mothers, many genetic legal fathers do not have PRRs automatically.

7 Presumption of paternity

In unassisted conception, the 1986 Act has two presumptions about who is the legal father and has PRRs. He automatically has PRRs and keeps them unless and until the presumption is rebutted in court proceedings and/or they are removed by a court order. A presumption is a general legal rule and may be challenged and rebutted by going to court and proving it untrue in a particular case. In cases about paternity, that is often shown by DNA evidence. The presumptions are:

- a man married to the mother or in a civil partnership at any time between the conception and the birth of a child is presumed to be the legal, genetic father or where the genetic father marries or enters into a civil partnership with the mother any time subsequently.
- a man not married to or in a civil partnership with the mother of a child is presumed to be the legal, genetic father *if* both he and the mother acknowledge him as the father *and* the child has been registered as his child in Scotland on or after 4 May 2006.

s.5 1986 Act; s.3 1995 Act, as amended by s.23 2006 Act

8 Establishing paternity in court

If there is a dispute about who is the father, a court can be asked to grant an order about paternity or non-paternity, called a Declarator. If a putative father obtains a Declarator of Paternity, this raises the presumption that he is the genetic father as if his name were on the birth certificate. While a Declarator of Paternity establishes parentage, it does not automatically confer PRRs.

Unmarried fathers may need to take additional steps to secure these rights through court orders or agreements with the child's mother.[26] However, if a man who is married to or in a civil partnership with the legal mother obtains a Declarator of Non-Paternity, this rebuts the presumption of paternity, and he loses the PRRs which he had.

s.7 1986 Act

9 Establishing paternity for children's hearings

Children's hearings may instruct a local authority to arrange that a DNA test is undertaken to establish paternity if it is in the child's best interests.

Appeal under s.154 of the Children's Hearings (Scotland) Act 2011 by JS Edinburgh [2021] Sc Edin 1

10 How fathers can acquire responsibilities and rights (PRRs)

10.1

A genetic father who does not have PRRs can acquire these by using the agreement provided for in s.4 of the 1995 Act. There is a straightforward form, which when signed by both genetic parents and sent for registration in the Books of Council and Session (a public register), gives the father full responsibilities and rights as if he had married the mother. There is a small cost for this, but no formal procedure is involved, and there is no need to go to court. Forms are available from organisations such as Citizens Advice Bureaux. However, they cannot be used by anyone who is not a genetic parent. Once this agreement is signed and registered, the couple cannot change their minds. The only way to alter the arrangements after that is to go to court.

s.4 1995 Act

26 https://www.mygov.scot/parental-responsibilities-rights/fathers

10.2

A father with no PRRs can also apply to court under s.11 of the 1995 Act to obtain them. He has to do this if the mother disagrees with his request for PRRs and refuses to sign a s.4 form. He may also apply to the court under s.11 if he wishes to acquire some PRRs, for example, in respect of contact. The paramountcy of the child's welfare will prevail in the court's decision-making.

s.11 1995 Act

11 Acquiring responsibilities and rights: Section 11 applications and orders

11.1

Section 11 of the 1995 Act allows courts (the sheriff court or Court of Session) to make any type of order about responsibilities and rights, guardianship or a child's property. The court can make an order because it has been asked to do so, or simply because, in any other case, it thinks an order is necessary.

s.11(1), (2) and (3) 1995 Act

The most common types of s.11 orders are:

- residence orders
- contact orders
- specific issue orders
- interdicts
- orders giving PRRs
- orders taking away some or all of a person's PRRs
- orders appointing or removing someone as a child's guardian

s.11(2) 1995 Act

11.2

Any person can use this section, provided they can claim an interest in the child (but see the restrictions on which orders the court may grant when a child is the subject of a permanence order or permanence order with authority to adopt). This includes all parents with PRRs, birth fathers without all or some of them and anyone else claiming an interest, including step-parents of children, whether married, civil partners, unmarried or same-sex partners. The only individuals who cannot apply under s.11 in this way are people who have already lost all their PRRs because of an adoption order or an order under the HFEA 1990 or 2008. However, where someone has lost PRRs because of an adoption order, they may apply for leave to apply for a contact order under s.11.

s.11 A 1995 Act inserted by the 2007 Act, s.103 and s.11(3)(aa) and (ab) and (4) as inserted and amended by the 2007 Act, s.107, Schedule 2, para 9(2) and Schedule 3

Local authorities cannot use this section, but children can use it, as well as adults.

s.11(5) 1995 Act

11.3

When a child is the subject of a permanence order or a permanence order with authority to adopt, a court may not make an order under s.11, unless the application is for an interdict, appointment of a judicial factor for the child or appointment or removal of someone as the child's guardian. This is because the permanence order or permanence order with authority to adopt will have set out who has what PRRs, and any changes should be applied for in a variation or revocation of the order.

1995 Act, s.11A inserted by the 2007 Act, s.103

11.4

The principles outlined in Chapter 2 apply to all s.11 decisions made by courts. This includes taking account of the child's religious persuasion, racial, cultural and linguistic heritage – see Chapter 2, paragraph 2.7.

s.11(7) and (10) 1995 Act

11.5

The law relating to children before the 1995 Act talked about "custody". The term in the 1995 Act is "residence" although it does *not* mean the same thing. A residence order may be granted to a parent who already has PRRs, *or* it may be granted to someone who does not have any responsibilities and rights to begin with, such as a grandparent or unmarried father.

s.11(12) 1995 Act

11.6

If a residence order is granted to a parent with PRRs, in a divorce or dissolution of civil partnership or other application, the order simply says where the child is to live. It does not take away some or all of the non-residential parent's PRRs, apart from residence, unless the court also orders this for particular reasons. The idea is to encourage parents to work together for their children. This means that the two parents with responsibilities are expected to continue to carry these out, even if they are separated or divorced, or their civil partnership has been dissolved. They both also retain rights.

s.11(11) 1995 Act

11.7

If a residence order is granted to a person who does not already have PRRs, the order allows that person to have all the responsibilities and rights that are needed to care properly for the child. It does not, however, take PRRs (except residence) away from anyone else who already has them, unless and only to the extent the court specifically orders.

s.11(11) and (12) 1995 Act

11.8

Because the principle of minimum necessary intervention applies in these decisions, courts should not grant orders to disputing parents just because parents want them. Courts have to be satisfied, taking the child's welfare as paramount, that the orders wanted are necessary for the child and that it is better to make the orders than not to do so. This represents a move away from giving custodial rights to one parent in a dispute and leaving the other parent with a feeling of very little involvement.

s.11(7)(a) 1995 Act

12 Interdicts and enforcement

12.1

As has already been mentioned, s.11 orders can include interdicts about children, including an interdict to prevent a child being removed from someone's care, if this is necessary to protect the child.

s.11(2)(f) 1995 Act

12.2

Certain orders made in Scotland in relation to children are recognised and may be enforced in other parts of the UK. Similarly, certain orders made elsewhere in the UK are also recognised and can be enforced in Scotland.

1986 Act

13 PRRs for children "looked after" by the local authority

13.1

The responsibilities of the local authorities themselves for looked after children are dealt with in Chapter 16. However, there is the issue of what parents' PRRs are when children are looked after by a local authority, either by arrangement under s.25 1995 Act or because of compulsory supervision orders from the children's hearing system or because there are permanence orders or permanence orders with authority to adopt. The position depends on the basis on which children are looked after.

13.2

Unlike the position in England and Wales in care orders under the 1989 Act, local authorities do *not* acquire any PRRs for looked after children except when they hold permanence orders or permanence orders with authority to adopt. For most looked after children, local authorities have no PRRs and this affects day-to-day issues for children, such as medical consent and holiday arrangements. Local authorities do have duties but not PRRs.

13.3

If a child is accommodated by the local authority, this is an arrangement between the local authority and the parents, and they do not lose PRRs. If they have any dispute with the local authority, they can ask for the child to be returned to them.

s.25 1995 Act

14 PRRs and the children's hearing system

14.1

If a child is subject to a compulsory supervision order in the hearing system, under ss.91 or 119 of the 2011 Act, the child may be at home or away from home. The PRRs are only affected to the extent that the local authority, as the Implementation Authority, has a duty to give effect to the compulsory supervision order and any measures attached to it. If a child is away from home on a compulsory supervision order, the parents' PRRs are moderated in relation to control of residence, and they cannot demand return of the child. The parents are not entitled to act in any way which is incompatible with the compulsory supervision order. When there is a compulsory supervision order for a child, arguably the courts cannot use s.11 to make orders about contact; only the children's hearing system can do this and any existing orders will be superseded by orders of the children's hearing.

s.3(4) 1995 Act, as amended by the Children's Hearings (Scotland) Act 2011 (Modification of Primary Legislation) Order 2013, SSI 2013/211; P v P 2000 SLT 781 (29 February 2000)

14.2

If someone wants to use s.11 to obtain a residence order for a child who is subject to a compulsory supervision order, the court may grant such an order, but the compulsory supervision order still takes precedence.

If the court grants an order to a carer named by the hearing system (e.g. a grandparent), then there is no conflict. If an order is granted to someone with whom the child does not live, it cannot be enforced unless and until the compulsory supervision order is terminated or varied to name that person.

s.3(4) 1995 Act as amended; P v P 2000 SLT 781 (29 February 2000)

15 Section 62 referrals

Any civil court in a wide range of cases, including adoption, permanence order and permanence order with authority to adopt applications, may refer a child to the Children's Reporter. The court specifies which s.67 grounds it thinks might apply. It is at the discretion of the Children's Reporter to decide whether to refer the child to a hearing. This is the way in which a court dealing with private law cases refers a child into the public law system if the court is concerned about the arrangements for the child (see Chapter 11 on the hearing system).

s.62 2011 Act

16 Acquiring PRRs in surrogacy

16.1

PRRs may be acquired in surrogacy by the application for parental orders, providing for a child to be treated in law as the child of the applicant/s.

16.2

The people who commission the surrogacy are often not legal parents and will usually have no PRRs. They may acquire these with the consent of the legal parent/s by a parental order under the HFEA 2008 if at least one of them is genetically related to the child. If there is no consent or no genetic relationship, they may seek adoption which may be granted even if money has been paid for the surrogacy.

s.54 HFEA 2008; s.29 2007 Act

16.3

If a legal father does not have PRRs, there are ways in which these can be obtained. If the other female parent under the 2008 Act does not have PRRs, these may be obtained by an agreement under s.4A or by an order under s.11 of the 1995 Act. Section 4A only applies in relation to assisted conception.

ss.33–35, 36, 37, 40, 42, 43, 44, 46 HFEA 2008, Part 2; s.3 1995 Act as amended by the 2008 Act, Schedule 6, para 50, s.4 and s.4A inserted by the 2008 Act, Schedule 6, para 51 and s.11

17 Application by two people

17.1

Where the pregnancy has occurred through artificial insemination of the gestational mother and one of the applicants is the biological parent of the child, a parental order can be made where the applicants are:

(a) *husband and wife,*

(b) *civil partners of each other, or*

(c) *two persons who are living as partners in an enduring family relationship and are not within prohibited degrees of relationship in relation to each other.*

17.2

There are several conditions to the granting of the application including that applicants must apply for the order within six months from the birth date, be resident with the child in Great Britain and over the age of 18. Consent must have been given by the gestational mother and non-parent applicants and no money or other benefit (other than for expenses reasonably incurred) has been given or received. The courts in Scotland and in England have not been prescriptive in applying these conditions. Where the application for a parenting order has not been made within six months of the child's birth; or where one of the applicants is dead and the other applicant is acting as their executor, courts have, nonetheless granted the orders.[27]

s.54 HFEA 2008

18 Application by one applicant

(1) One person may apply to the court for the child to be treated as their child in law, where the gestational mother became pregnant using the gametes of the applicant.

The same conditions apply as with two applicants except, of course, in respect of their relationship.

s.54A HFEA 2008

27 *AB and XY Petitioners [2023] CSOH 40, 2023 SLT 893; Re X (A Child) [2014] EWHC 3135 (Fam);* A v P *[2011] EWHC 1738 (Fam)*

19 Motherhood: where there are two women with a biological claim to motherhood

1. The woman whose egg created the embryo – the biological mother, and 2. the woman who carried the baby during pregnancy – the gestational mother – she alone is to be treated as the legal mother of the child.

The gestational mother has the same legal rights in respect of the child as a mother who conceived without assisted reproduction.

s.33 HFEA 2008

20 Fatherhood

20.1

While the gestational mother is the legal mother, the rules about who is the legal father or other parent are extremely complex and this is just a basic outline.

20.2

To acquire PRRs, men become fathers under the assisted reproduction legislation depending on consent where it is not his sperm that is being used. Fatherhood is conferred on the basis of consent to the woman's insemination/ treatment. This is where the distinction is drawn between a married and unmarried father.

20.3

Consent of a married man is presumed. He is the father unless he can prove that he did not consent – effectively an "opt out" system.

s.35 HFEA 2008

20.4

If he is unmarried, he has to formally consent to the treatment for him to be the father, i.e. "opting in". However, for him to be able to opt in, the woman must be artificially inseminated in the course of treatment provided by a licensed, registered clinic within the UK.

ss.35 and 36 HFEA 2008

21 2nd legal parent

21.1

The 2008 Act introduced the 2nd legal parent in same-sex relationships, for each woman to be recognised as the legal parent of the child. The same presumptions prevail as above, namely if the women are married or in a legal partnership, their consent to being the 2nd legal parent is presumed.

s.42 HFEA 2008

21.2

Where they are not married or in a civil partnership, the 2nd parent's consent is needed. Again, this opting in can only happen where the woman was artificially inseminated in the course of treatment provided by a licensed, registered clinic within the UK.

ss.43 and 44 HFEA 2008

22 Deceased donor

If a woman conceives using sperm or an embryo from a deceased donor, the child has no legal father or other parent, although the deceased may be registered as the father for registration purposes only.

5

Rights of siblings

This chapter looks at the rights of siblings and duties of local authorities, courts and children's hearings in the promotion and support of sibling relationships. Legislation codified existing good practice in recognising and promoting the sibling relationship where appropriate.

Legislation reinforces the importance of the sibling relationship and the local authority's obligation in supporting and promoting sibling relationships for **care experienced children**.

2020 Act, LAC(S) Amendment Regs 2021

Definition of sibling:

- Brothers and sisters who share at least one parent.
- Any other person with whom the child has lived or is living, and with whom the child has an ongoing relationship, with the character of a relationship between siblings.

s.13(2)(b) 2020 Act

1 Sibling and sibling like relationship

A sibling relationship can be wider than a biological brother or sister, including full, half, step and adopted siblings, and include sibling like relationships. This might be influenced by who a child sees as their sibling as well as being an objective assessment of the relationship. For example, if a child is brought up in the same household as their cousin, that could be a sibling like relationship. If a child shared a room with another child in a foster home for one occasion overnight, that would not.

All siblings capable of giving a view to a local authority should be enabled to do so.

2 Placement of siblings

Where the local authority is considering placing a child with a kinship carer, foster carer or in a residential establishment and the child's sibling is looked after or about to be looked after, the local authority must, where appropriate, place the child and the sibling of the child with the same carer or in the same residential establishment.

Where this cannot happen, the siblings must be placed in homes which are near to each other. A local authority may only place a child in homes that are near together rather than in the same placement if that better safeguards and promotes the welfare of the child. Local authorities must seek and take account of siblings' views in relation to carrying out their assessment and the formulation of each child's plan.

Regs 3 and 4 – Looked After Children (Scotland) Amendment Regulations 2021 inserting Reg 5A Looked After Children (Scotland) Act 2009

3 Maximum number of children in a foster placement

The Looked After Children (Scotland) Amendment Regulations 2014 introduced a limit to the number of unrelated children who could reside in one fostering placement. One of the exceptions to this rule is where there is a group of more than three siblings. The amendment allows for this to last for longer than the previous maximum amount of time. The local authority must refer the child to the fostering panel within four weeks of the placement or as soon as practicable thereafter. The panel will review whether this is an acceptable arrangement.

Reg 3 (27A) – Looked After Children (Scotland) Amendment Regulations 2021

4 Independent Care Review 2020 – The Promise

> *Where living with their family is not possible, children must stay with their*

brothers and sisters where safe to do so and belong to a loving home, staying there for as long as needed.

There will always be some children who cannot stay with their families. Some will need to be away from their family for a short time, others will never live with their family again while many return later and as young adults.

There is already the presumption that children will stay together with their brothers and sisters if they have to be removed from their family. This is a significant step in nurturing vital loving relationships. Brothers and sisters keep each other safe and loved. There will be few circumstances where it is not appropriate for brothers and sisters to stay together, but these will be the exception.

(The Promise, p.19)

5 Promotion of contact between looked after children and siblings

The local authority has a duty to promote on a regular basis, personal relations and direct contact between "siblings" as appear to them to be appropriate. This means that the new legislation provides for siblings of a looked after child to have a more unfettered right to contact with the child than that of the child's parents where the local authority's duty applies only where it is appropriate and practicable.

In respect of looked after children, the local authority shall safeguard and promote the child's welfare which shall, in the exercise of their duty to the child, be their paramount concern.

s.13 2020 Act amending s.17 Children (Scotland) Act 1995

6 Taking account of the child's views in maintaining sibling relationships

6.1

Local authorities should discover and monitor a looked after child's wishes about continuing contact with their parents and other family members. The views of each child should be ascertained, as far as is possible given their age and understanding. The local authority should, with the agency's help, keep the child's contact with their family under review. Siblings fall within the category of family members.

6.2

Both in the early stages of placement and for children who spend prolonged periods looked after away from home by a local authority, contact with siblings living elsewhere and with other extended family members and friends needs similar attention as contact with parents. This should be recognised in its own right and not purely as part of contact with parents.

6.3

The guidance goes on to emphasise the need for the local authority to maintain as much as possible "familiar and comforting relationships". It may be appropriate for frequent contact to be maintained.

6.4

The regulation uses 'any other child in the same family' rather than sibling. This highlights the need for awareness of who the child views as their "siblings". Many families have complex structures with full, half and step-siblings and research shows that children's perception of brothers and sisters and who is in their family is rooted as much in living experience as biological connectedness.

Guidance on Looked After Child (Scotland) Regulations 2009, p.42

7 Duty to consider contact when making a compulsory supervision order

Children's hearings and courts must consider, when making a compulsory supervision order, a measure to regulate contact not only with a relevant person, but also with a sibling, as defined within the Act.

s.14(3) 2020 Act modifying s.29A 2011 Act

8 Participation rights of brothers and sisters in children's hearings

8.1

These rights will apply where the sibling:

- is living with or has lived with the child;
- there is an ongoing sibling like relationship with the child;
- the children's hearing is likely to make a decision that would significantly affect when or how the sibling has contact with the child, or if there is a possibility of having contact;
- the sibling is able to give views on when or how they see the child.

The rights are:

- to be notified of the hearing;
- to provide a report for the hearing;
- to receive some of the hearing papers;
- to be allowed to attend for part of the hearing;
- to have a representative at the hearing;
- to request a review of a compulsory supervision order after three months.

8.2

Other reviews open to siblings will only be arranged where the sibling asks the Reporter to arrange them. This could occur in the following circumstances:

- If the sibling had participation rights but did not attend the children's hearing, they might be able to have a review before three months. This can happen where the sibling was not able to participate properly because of a procedural failure or because of exceptional circumstances.
- If the sibling did not have participation rights and did not attend the children's hearing, they might be able to have a review before three months. This can happen where there was no decision by a children's hearing or pre-hearing panel about whether the sibling had participation rights and a children's hearing or pre-hearing panel – if it had considered it – would likely have decided that the sibling did have participation rights.

9 Case law clarifying the rights of siblings in children's hearings

The judgements in these cases restated the importance of sibling relationships in the decision making of children's hearings involving looked after children and their siblings.

ABC (Appellant) v Principal Reporter and another (Respondents) (Scotland) In the matter of XY (Appellant) (Scotland) [2020] UKSC 26; Decision of the Court in MB v Principal Reporter [2021] CSOH 19; 16 February 2021 Lady Wise

10 Seeking a contact order through the courts

Anyone can apply to the court to grant a contact order in relation to a child. This means that a sibling can seek this formal arrangement to secure contact with their sibling, even where they are not looked after. The court's primary consideration continues to be the welfare of each child for whom they are asked to make a decision. This, along with the minimum intervention and taking account of the child's views, represent the cornerstones to any court decision in relation to children.

s.11(2)(d) 1995 Act

11 Views of siblings in adoption

11.1

There is a general duty on the court and adoption agency where they are coming to a decision relating to the adoption of a child to take into account the views of the parents, guardians and other relatives of the child. This will, by definition, include siblings.

s.14(5) 2007 Act

11.2

There is a similar general duty in notifying within seven days of making the decision that adoption is in the child's best interests any other relative of the child who has expressed a view on the placement of the child for adoption to the adoption agency.

Reg 14(1)(e) Adoption Agencies (Scotland) Regulations 2009

6

The Disclosure system for criminal record checks, the PVG Scheme and vetting and barring

The principle underpinning the disclosure of information about an individual's criminal record is the balance between an individual's right to privacy under Article 8 of the ECHR and the State's responsibility for agencies to comply with their duty to protect children and young people. Decisions made by the agency about what action to take arising from information coming out of a disclosure check will need to be proportionate and justifiable, showing how the agency has balanced the rights of children to be protected with the adult's rights.

1 Disclosure Scotland

The Police Act 1997 introduced a new system for disclosing criminal history information to individuals and organisations for employment and other purposes. Disclosure Scotland is the body that arranges for checks.

Police Act 1997; Rehabilitation of Offenders Act 1974

2 Different levels of Disclosure checks

Disclosure Scotland provides Enhanced, Standard and Basic Disclosures under the 1997 Act.

- An **Enhanced Disclosure** contains all conviction information – relevant spent or unspent under the Rehabilitation of Offenders Act 1974, and any other non-conviction information considered relevant by the police or other Government bodies – Other Relevant Information ("ORI"). It also discloses information about Barred Lists and from the Sex Offenders Register. Enhanced disclosures are used for:
    - Work carried out in a prison (wholly or partly).
    - Individuals being assessed as suitable for adopting a child.
    - Adult residing in the same household as foster carers, child minders or individuals being assessed as suitable for adopting a child.
- A **Standard Disclosure** contains all conviction information, relevant spent and unspent, including cautions, but no non-conviction information or police intelligence. It also discloses information held on the Sex Offenders Register. Standard Disclosures are only available for:
    - Certain "exempted" professions (accountant, solicitor, "allied" health professions, vets, taxi/private hire driver, most roles governed by the Financial Conduct Authority).
    - Any employment concerned with the provision of a care service (e.g. admin, receptionist).
    - Any employment concerned with the provision of health service that involves contact with patients, etc.
- A **Basic Disclosure** contains only convictions unspent under the 1974 Act. Basic Disclosures:
    - May be applied for by anyone and it can be used for any purpose.
    - If the request is from an employer, the applicant's consent is required.
    - Individuals can apply online via the Disclosure Scotland website: www.mygov.scot/basic-disclosure/apply-for-basic-disclosure

While anyone can apply for a Basic Disclosure for themself, enhanced and standard disclosures may only be applied for by organisations and those entitled to seek them for people doing certain work or holding certain posts.

3 Code of Practice

There is a Code of Practice in connection with the use of disclosure information provided to registered persons and counter-signatories and in the discharge of any functions by those registered persons and counter-signatories under the 1997 Act and under the Protection of Vulnerable Groups (Scotland) Act 2007 ("the 2007 Act"). The Code was last updated in 2023.

Disclosure Scotland Code of Practice: www.mygov.scot

4 To whom the Code applies

The Code applies to the following persons who must comply with The Code:

- any person registered under s.120 of the 1997 Act, including bodies corporate and unincorporate, statutory office-holders, employers and umbrella bodies;
- any employees or agents of registered persons, nominated by these bodies for the purpose of countersigning applications or making PVG declarations in relation to disclosure requests on behalf of them;
- any employee or individual in a third-party organisation that has received disclosure information from an umbrella body that has countersigned an application or made a PVG declaration on behalf of that third-party organisation;
- recipients in the Scottish Administration or other Government departments, of disclosure information provided under ss.114 and 116 of the 1997 Act in connection with Crown employment or judicial appointments.

The Code does not apply to the individual who is the subject of the disclosure information.

5 Purpose of the Code

The Code is intended to:

- ensure that disclosure information, released by Disclosure Scotland to registered persons and counter-signatories, is used properly and lawfully by those persons;
- provide assurance to those individuals applying for either a standard or an enhanced disclosure under the 1997 Act or making a disclosure request under the 2007 Act that disclosure information will be used properly and lawfully by registered persons and counter-signatories;
- ensure that disclosure information is handled and stored appropriately by registered persons and is kept for only as long as necessary for the purpose it was requested and thereafter disposed of securely.

6 Obligations under the Code

There are a number of specific statutory requirements with which registered persons and/or counter signatories must comply. Those relate to: the provision of registration information; ensuring disclosure applications and requests are made and used in accordance with the law; and data obligations in respect of the handling and storing of disclosure information which should be kept for only as long as necessary for the purpose it was requested and thereafter disposed of securely.

7 Protection of Vulnerable Groups: PVG Scheme

7.1

In 2011, the system of criminal record checks and listing was extended to include those working with protected adults when the POCSA 2003 was repealed and replaced by the PVG(S)A 2007. Consequently, there are two separate lists, for people considered unsuitable to work with children and/or with protected adults. The Act introduced the PVG Scheme for vetting people working with children and protected adults and barring those on one or other of the lists. There are also duties on organisations to refer people for possible inclusion on one or other of the lists.

PVG(S)A 2007

7.2

Disclosure Scotland provides PVG Scheme disclosures under the PVG(S)A 2007, for Scheme members. Many people are required to have a criminal record check when "working" with children (under the age of 18), in both paid employment or on a voluntary basis. A list is to be kept by Scottish Ministers of people unsuitable to work with children; and there are duties on courts, employers, voluntary organisations and others to refer people for possible listing.

If someone is barred from regulated work, Disclosure Scotland does not issue a PVG.

7.3

The PVG Scheme registers an organisation as an Interested Party to the individual and entitles the organisation to updates through Continuous Monitoring.

7.4

The PVG Scheme discloses:

- unspent convictions
- relevant spent convictions
- Sex Offenders Register
- other relevant information ("ORI")
- information about Barred Lists

Police Act 1997, Part V; PVG(S)A 2007

8 Continuous monitoring of Scheme members

Ongoing monitoring is a key component of the PVG Scheme. Every PVG Scheme member is monitored during their membership, and this starts upon the completion of their application to join the PVG Scheme.

Disclosure Scotland keeps checking their suitability to continue working with children and protected adults. These record updates and membership statements issued after joining can be carried out without the need to apply for a new full disclosure every time; and for automatic updating of the Scheme member's record if any new vetting information arises.

All new conviction information on police systems is fed in automatically and associated with relevant PVG membership accounts, with an average of 40,000 updates per day. Where Disclosure Scotland finds new information that amounts to an unsuitability to work with children or protected adults, they will bar that person from regulated work. They will also remove the person from the PVG Scheme and tell any employers listed on the account of the bar.

PVG(S)A 2007

9 Regulated Work assessment

The **PVG Scheme** involves assessing whether an individual is doing **Regulated Work**. There are **five steps** to help organisations determine eligibility for regulated work:

1. Is it work?
2. Who are they working with?
   Are they working with children or protected adults?
3. What are they doing?
   Is the work considered regulated work? Are they working in a regulated establishment?

4. Is it a normal duty?
   Or is the regulated activity "Incidental"?
5. Are there any exceptions?
   Supervisor or line manager
   Positions of trust
   Employees under 18

10 Disclosure (Scotland) Act 2020

Parts of the Act have already been implemented and other changes were implemented in 2024.

The Act makes some important amendments to the operation of the PVG Scheme, but the ethos and obligations under the Scheme remain.

The improvements to the PVG scheme and safeguarding in Scotland include:

- Simpler disclosure products, including a timed PVG membership.
- Replacing the concept of "Regulated work" with "Regulated roles" to make it more easily understood.
- The PVG Scheme is becoming mandatory for those carrying out "regulated roles" with children and protected adults.
- Ability for Disclosure Scotland to impose conditions on PVG Scheme members who are under consideration for listing.

11 Criminal record checks in fostering

Criminal record checks must be undertaken on prospective foster carers.

Applications are made for prospective foster carers to become members of the PVG Scheme and Scheme membership for as long as they remain approved.

Criminal record checks must also be undertaken on anyone aged 16 and over who is a household member of the prospective foster carers.

These checks are provided under the Police Act 1997 and applications are made for "Enhanced disclosures: children suitability checks". They are not eligible for PVG Scheme membership.

LAC(S) Regs 2009 Schedule 3. Paras 2 and 10

12 Criminal records checks in adoption

Criminal record checks are required to be undertaken on prospective adopters and all household members who are aged 16 and over. This also applies to intercountry prospective adopters.

Applications are made for "Enhanced disclosure: children suitability checks", and they are not eligible for the PVG Scheme membership.

However, where prospective adopters are also being assessed as foster carers, these checks are provided under the PVG Scheme, and prospective adopters are treated as foster carers by Disclosure Scotland.

Adoption Agencies (Scotland) Regulations 2009; s.7 and Schedule 1, Part 1 paras 9 and 14(f)(g)

7

The 2010 Act and the Care Inspectorate

1 Legislation

This chapter deals with the Public Services Reform (Scotland) Act 2010, which made significant changes to the organisation of public services in Scotland. It streamlined the structure of various bodies, transferring functions from one organisation to another. Ministerial functions were delegated to improve efficiency and decision-making in public services. By reorganising and simplifying public bodies, the Act sought to enhance service delivery, reduce bureaucracy and improve accountability.

The Act contains regulatory and inspection systems, substituting the Care Commission with the Care Inspectorate for many matters.

The Act means that people working in social services have to adhere to established rules and codes of practice. Failing to comply with the Act and associated regulations means they can be de-registered, meaning that they will no longer be able to provide social care services.

2 The 2001 and the 2010 Acts: the Care Inspectorate

The 2010 Act covers a wide range of public authorities and established two bodies: the Social Care and Social Work Improvement Scotland (SCSWIS) (otherwise the Care Inspectorate), and Health Improvement Scotland (HIS), to regulate health matters.

Part 5, ss.44–107 and Part 6, ss.108–110; see particularly ss.44, 52 and 108 2010 Act

3 The Care Inspectorate

The Care Inspectorate was set up in April 2011 by the Scottish Government as a scrutiny body for the regulation, registration and inspection of all the care services in Scotland listed in the 2010 Act.

It deals with complaints about services and enforcement of Standards and conditions. The Care Inspectorate also has a general duty to improve the quality of "social services", which means "care services" and "social work services". The latter are local authorities and other social work services listed in Schedule 13.

Part 5, esp. ss.45–48, 50 and 51, and 53–92, and Schedules 12 and 13 2010 Act

4 Care services

4.1

There are 13 "care services" listed in s.47(1), with the detailed definitions set out in Schedule 12. They include support services, care home services, secure accommodation services, adoption services, fostering services, childminding and day care of children. Some are only provided for children, like adoption, fostering and day care, but others are for all ages, like care homes.

s.47 and Schedule 12, 2010 Act

4.2

All the care services listed must be registered with and inspected by the Care Inspectorate. For registration, there are general provisions for all care services except local authority adoption and fostering, which are covered by other sections. There are general provisions for inspections of all care services.

ss.59 and 83 and ss.53–58 2010 Act

5 Health and Social Care Standards 2018

5.1

As part of the system of registration and inspection, Scottish ministers are obliged to publish care standards for the various care services. These were updated in 2018 with Scotland's Health and Social Care Standards[28] and replace the 23 sets of standards produced for different types of registered care settings introduced in 2002.

5.2

The Care Inspectorate is required, by law, to consider the Health and Social Care Standards when making decisions about registrations, during inspections and other scrutiny and improvement work.

The Standards are a set of standards for care services in Scotland. They are underpinned by five principles: dignity and respect, compassion, be included, responsive care, and support and wellbeing. They aim to improve the quality of life and outcomes for service users by ensuring consistent and high-quality care across Scotland.[29]

They have five keynote outcomes:

- I experience high quality care and support that is right for me.
- I am fully involved in all decisions about my care and support.
- I have confidence in the people who support and care for me.
- I have confidence in the organisation providing my care and support.
- I experience a high quality environment if the organisation provides the premises.

s.50 2010 Act

28 https://www.gov.scot/publications/health-social-care-standards-support-life/
29 https://en.wikipedia.org/wiki/National_Care_Standards_(Scotland)

5.3

The main care standards relating to children in Quality Frameworks include:

- Daycare of children, childminding and school-aged childcare
- Children and young people in need of care and protection
- Mainstream boarding schools and school hostels
- Secure accommodation services
- Fostering, adoption and adult placement services
- Care homes for children and young people and school care accommodation
- Support services (care at home, including supported living models of support)
- Support services (not care at home)

These are available through the Care Commission's website in their quality frameworks and KQ7s.[30]

6 The Scottish Social Services Council

6.1

The Council is responsible for the registration in Scotland of people who work in social services, and for regulating their education and training. Qualified social workers, i.e. those with a Diploma in Social Work (DipSW) or equivalent qualification, must be registered on the Register of Social Service Workers in Scotland in order to practice as social workers.

ss.44 and 52 2001 Act

30 https://www.careinspectorate.com/index.php/publications-statistics/147-professionals-registration/quality-frameworks?start=10

6.2

The Council must also promote high standards of behaviour and practice among social services workers and in education and training. There are UK-wide Codes developed by the Council and the equivalent regulatory bodies in the rest of the UK. The SSSC Codes of Practice (the Codes) set out:

- the standards of practice and behaviour expected of everyone who works in social services in Scotland.
- the standards expected of employers of social service workers in Scotland.

All workers and employers are expected to adhere to the Codes.

ss.43 and 53 2001 Act

7 New Codes of Practice

In May 2024, the codes were revised. The two sets of Codes continue to mirror the responsibilities of both employers and workers in meeting the standards those using their services can expect as well as society in general.

7.1 Code of Practice for Social Service Workers

- I must protect and promote the rights and interests of individuals and carers.
- I must build and maintain the trust and confidence of individuals and carers.
- I must promote the wellbeing and independence of individuals and carers while protecting them, as far as possible from harm.
- I must recognise that individuals have the right to take risks and will work with them to understand and manage those risks.
- I must be accountable for the quality of my work and take responsibility for maintaining and improving my knowledge and skills.

- I must uphold public trust and confidence.

7.2 Code of Practice for Employers of Social Service Workers

Make sure people you recruit are suitable to be social service workers and that they understand their roles and responsibilities.

- Maintain a culture and have systems in place to support social service workers to meet their Code of Practice.
- Provide learning and development opportunities to enable workers to strengthen and maintain their skills, knowledge and practice.
- Maintain a culture that supports safety and protection while respecting the rights of individuals to take risks.
- Publicise and promote the Code of Practice for Social Service Employers and the Code of Practice for Social Service Workers to individuals and carers and cooperate with SSSC proceedings.

8

Private care arrangements

This chapter deals with private care arrangements which parents and families may make for their children at home, or with relatives or with other people. Childminding and day care of children are regulated by the 2010 Act.

1 Arrangements at home

If parents make arrangements directly with a carer for babysitting or childcare in their own home, *without* the involvement of a child care agency, there are no controls over these. The 2010 Act does not cover such arrangements. However, a carer and/or the parents could be liable criminally if the arrangements are inadequate.

s.12 1937 Act

2 Carers' responsibilities in respect of a child

When carers for children do not have parental responsibilities and rights (PRRs), they still have a general duty to safeguard the children's welfare. Carers may also be able to consent to medical treatment in certain circumstances: carers must be at least 16, the children must be unable to consent and the carers should have no reason to believe that the parents would refuse to consent.

s.5 1995 Act

3 Leaving children unattended

It is not an offence to leave children under 16 unattended, but if harm or neglect is suffered by the children, the people who left them unattended may be charged with a criminal offence. This applies to parents and any other carers who are 16 or over.

s.12 1937 Act

4 Arrangements with family

If parents make arrangements for a child to be cared for by a close relative, there is no regulatory control or involvement. If the relative is not a close one and the care is for less than 28 days, there is still no regulatory control. If the care is for more than 28 days, then it will be a private fostering arrangement and the local authority must be notified.

5 Childminding

5.1

Childminding is one of the care services listed in the 2010 Act. Childminders must therefore register with the Care Inspectorate. There are conditions in regulations for registration and it may be refused. There is an annual registration and inspection fee. In addition, the Care Inspectorate must inspect the premises which are used for childminding and the arrangements.

s.47 and Schedule 12, paras 12 and 14, s.59 and Part 5 generally 2010 Act

5.2

Childminding is the provision of childcare in a domestic setting. Childminding is defined as 'looking after one or more children on domestic premises for reward for a period of more than two hours in any day'.

This does not include caring for closely related children; foster children or caring for children in their own home.

Schedule 12, paras 12 and 14 2010 Act

6 Maximum number of children receiving care

The framework that applies to childminding is the Quality Improvement framework for early learning and childcare sectors.[31] It states that one childminder may provide care for no more than six children under the age of 12. Of those six children, three or fewer must not be attending primary school and no more than one is under the age of 12 months. These numbers include the childminder's own children; this means all children of the childminder's family whether or not they are present. For example, if a child of the family is at nursery or school or with a relative, they are still counted in the numbers.

Part 5 of the 2010 Act sets out Regulations that must be complied with by childminders. These Regulations set out requirements that must be complied with by providers of care services, which includes childminders.

7 Nanny

A nanny is not a childminder if they are looking after a child in the home of their employer. However, if they have been supplied or introduced to the parents by a child care agency, that is a child care agency service, which is regulated by the 2001 Act.

Schedule 12, paras 5 and 12(3) 2010 Act

8 Day care

8.1

Day care is a care service under the 2010 Act. It is defined in the 2010 Act as a service providing:

> *...any form of care (whether or not provided to any extent in the form of an educational activity), supervised by a responsible person and not excepted*

31 https://www.careinspectorate.com/index.php/quality-improvement-framework-for-early-learning-and-childcare-sectors

from this definition by regulations, provided for children, on premises other than domestic premises, during the day (whether or not it is provided on a regular basis or commences or ends during the hours of daylight).

8.2

Providers must register with the Care Inspectorate, which may impose certain conditions. These include specifying the number of children who may be cared for and the number of helpers. Registration may be refused or cancelled. The Care Inspectorate must inspect day services.

s.47 and Schedule 12, paras 13–18, s.59 and Part 5 generally 2010 Act

8.3

Day care can include nursery classes, crèches, after-school groups and playgroups. They may be run by the public, private or voluntary sectors. The Quality Framework is Day care of children, childminding and school-aged childcare.

9 Child care agencies

9.1

Child care agencies are a care service defined originally in the 2001 Act and now in the 2010 Act. They are services 'supplying, or introducing to persons who use the service, child carers' to look after children up to the age of 16, wholly or mainly in their homes, and 'whether or not for reward and whether on a day-to-day or on an occasional basis'. They may include nanny agencies, home-based child care services and sitter services. The agencies may be managed by private, voluntary or local authority providers.

Schedule 12, para 5 2010 Act

9.2

The supply or introduction of child carers through a child care agency was previously regulated under the 2001 Act but now applies instead under provisions of the 2010 Act. Agencies must register with the Care Inspectorate, which may impose certain conditions. Registration may be refused or cancelled. The Care Inspectorate must inspect child care agencies.

s.47 and Schedule 12, para 5, s.59 and Part 5 generally 2010 Act

9.3

When parents enter into arrangements directly with a child carer for babysitting or child care in their home, without involving an agency, the arrangements are not subject to regulation under the 2010 Act.

10 Private fostering

Private fostering is care of a child provided:

- by an individual who is *not* a close relative; and
- on a private basis by arrangement between the parents and the individual; and
- for a period of 28 days or more.

Private fostering is covered by the 1984 Act and the 1985 Regs. It must be distinguished from public foster care arranged by the local authority, where the local authority makes such arrangements and places a child with approved foster carers. Public fostering makes a child a "looked after" child. Public and private fostering are both dealt with in later chapters.

1985 Regs, 1984 Act

9

Orders and national guidance for child protection

This chapter briefly outlines the child protection system and the three court orders used for the purposes of child protection, in the 1995 and 2011 Acts.

1 Child protection

> *Child protection refers to the processes involved in consideration, assessment and planning of required action, together with the actions themselves, where there are concerns that a child may be at risk of harm. Child protection guidance provides overall direction for agencies and professional disciplines where there are concerns that a child may be at risk of harm.*

(*National Guidance for Child Protection in Scotland 2021* (updated 2023), para 1.50)

2 Guidance

Most of the child protection system is organised on the basis of guidance from the Scottish Government and is not contained in statutes. Guidance sets out the multi-agency collaborative approach that must be taken by practitioners in local authorities including social work and education, those in the third sector, health and police. A national framework contains protocols, training, plans and procedures to support local interagency forums and provide consistency.

The 2021 guidance revised previous guidance to reflect changes in child protection legislation, standards, policy, practice, research and findings from learning reviews. This was reviewed and updated in 2023.

National Guidance for Child Protection in Scotland 2021 (updated 2023)

3 Child assessment orders (CAOs)

3.1

This order was introduced in 1995 and continued into the 2011 Act.

It allows local authorities (and only local authorities) to apply to the sheriff to grant an order for an assessment of:

(a) the child's health or development, or

(b) the way in which the child has been or is being treated or neglected.

The sheriff has to be satisfied that:

(a) the local authority has reasonable cause to suspect –

(i) that the child has been or is being treated in such a way that the child is suffering or is likely to suffer significant harm, or

(ii) that the child has been or is being neglected and as a result of the neglect the child is suffering or is likely to suffer significant harm,

[and]

(b) an assessment [of the type mentioned above] is necessary in order to establish whether there is reasonable cause to believe that the child has been or is being so treated or neglected, and

(c) it is unlikely that the assessment could be carried out, or carried out satisfactorily, unless the order was made.

ss.35 and 36 2011 Act

3.2

The order can last for a maximum of three days and must specify the period for which it has effect. It can authorise the production of the child to anyone for the purposes of assessment and taking the child to any place for the assessment. It can allow any type of assessment. One obvious use is for medical assessment, but the order is not restricted to that.

s.35 2011 Act

3.3

There are no regulations regarding these orders and the child is not looked after by the local authority.

3.4

There are court rules about applying for child assessment orders. Notice is given to the child's family, as ordered by the sheriff. Child assessment orders may, however, be obtained on fairly short notice. If parents wish to oppose an application for an order, they appear before the sheriff, who hears both sides of the application.

AS 1997, r.3.13(2) and rr.3.25–3.28, and general provisions, rr.3.1–3.24, all as amended for the 2011 Act

3.5

When a child assessment order application is made, a sheriff may grant a child protection order instead of a child assessment order, if they think that the conditions for a child protection order are satisfied.

s.36(3) 2011 Act

4 Child protection orders (CPOs)

4.1

Under the 1995 Act, this order replaced the "place of safety" formerly obtained under s.37 of the 1968 Act. It was therefore not a new remedy, but the procedures were different from those under the 1968 Act. It has now been moved to the 2011 Act.

ss.37–54 2011 Act

4.2

Anyone may apply for a child protection order, including local authorities. Almost all applications are by local authorities. All applications must go to the sheriff. There are two different tests depending on who is applying.

4.3

If an application is made by "any person" (including the local authority), the sheriff may grant the order if satisfied that:

(a) *there are reasonable grounds to believe that –*

- (i) *the child has been or is being treated in such a way that the child is suffering or is likely to suffer significant harm, [or]*
- (ii) *the child has been or is being neglected and as a result of the neglect the child is suffering or is likely to suffer significant harm, [or]*
- (iii) *the child is likely to suffer significant harm if the child is not removed to and kept in a place of safety, or*
- (iv) *the child is likely to suffer significant harm if the child does not remain in the place at which the child is staying (whether or not the child is resident there), and*

(b) *the order is necessary to protect the child from that harm or from further harm.*

s.39 2011 Act

4.4

If an application is made by a local authority, they may either satisfy the above test or the one in s.38. The sheriff may grant the order if satisfied that:

(a) *the local authority has reasonable grounds to suspect that –*

(i) the child has been or is being treated in such a way that the child is suffering or is likely to suffer significant harm, [or]

(ii) the child has been or is being neglected and as a result of the neglect the child is suffering or is likely to suffer significant harm, or

(iii) the child will be treated or neglected in such a way that is likely to cause significant harm to the child, [and]

(b) *the local authority is making enquiries to allow it to decide whether to take action to safeguard the welfare of the child, or is causing those enquiries to be made, [and]*

(c) *those enquiries are being frustrated by access to the child being unreasonably denied, and*

(d) *the local authority has reasonable cause to believe that access is required as a matter of urgency.*

s.38 2011 Act

4.5

A local authority may use either test, but anyone else can only use the test in s.39.

4.6

Again, there are court rules about applying for child protection orders. They are dealt with on an emergency basis and it is not mandatory to give advance notice to the family, although some sheriffs require this in some cases. If the sheriff is satisfied and grants an order, the local authority or other applicant must immediately serve on or give the family a copy of the order. This should be done when they remove the child or tell the family that the child is not being removed from the place of safety where they already are. A copy of the order will also be sent to the child, unless the sheriff decides this is not appropriate, given the child's age and maturity.

rr.3.29–3.33, and general provisions, rr.3.1–3.24, AS 1997 all as amended for the 2011 Act

4.7

If a child protection order is granted, the child does not become a looked after child. However, if the child is removed to a place of safety under the order, the local authority has the same duties to them as if they are looked after. Also, the child must be referred immediately to the Children's Reporter, who must decide whether they will take the case forward to a children's hearing. There are complicated rules about times within which hearings must be held, and failure to stick to the rules means that the child protection order will fall. Decisions about whether the child continues to be subject to the child protection order are made by the children's hearing members and/or the sheriff, depending on whether the family exercises its rights to ask the sheriff to reconsider the case. A child protection order lasts for a maximum of eight working days. At the end of that time, if the case is proceeding, there must be a hearing at which s.67 grounds for referral are put and a decision made as to whether the child is to continue to be "away from home" on an interim compulsory supervision order.

ss.43–54 2011 Act

4.8 Emergency protection

There are arrangements for sheriffs to be available for child protection order applications to be heard at any time, including out of hours. If, however, a local authority or other persons are unable to present an application to a sheriff, they may seek emergency protection from a Justice of the Peace. The Justice has to be satisfied on the same terms as the sheriff, and also 'that it is not practicable in the circumstances' for a sheriff to deal with the matter. If such emergency protection is obtained, it falls after 12 hours if not implemented. In any case, it may only last for a maximum of 24 hours, by which time the matter must be put before a sheriff with a child protection order application, unless the child goes home.

s.55 2011 Act

4.9

The police have a similar power to give emergency protection for up to 24 hours.

s.56 2011 Act

5 Exclusion orders (EOs)

5.1

Like child protection orders and child assessment orders, exclusion orders were introduced by the 1995 Act and represented a new remedy. They have not been moved to the 2011 Act and remain in the 1995 Act. They allow a person to be removed from the family home if the child is at risk, as an alternative to removing the child from home. Only a local authority may apply and the application must be made to a sheriff.

5.2

The sheriff must be satisfied that:

- the child has suffered, is suffering or is likely to suffer "significant harm" because of the behaviour, threats, etc. of "a person"; and
- that it is necessary to make an exclusion order against the "a person" to protect the child, this being a better safeguard for the child than taking them away from home; and

- that if the order is made, there will be an "appropriate person" in the house to care for the child and anyone else there.

s.76(2) 1995 Act

5.3

Again, there are court rules about these applications. An application for an exclusion order may either be on an "emergency basis", without notice, or be heard after notice has been given to the family.

rr.3.34–3.40 AS 1997

5.4

A sheriff may grant an interim exclusion order without giving notice to the "named person", but it may be difficult to satisfy a sheriff that this should be done.

s.76(4) 1995 Act

5.5

Another practical difficulty is that the local authority, in applying for the order, and the sheriff, in granting it, have to be satisfied that there is an "appropriate person" and that they will fully protect the child and anyone else in the house, and not simply allow the "named person" back into the house.

s.76(2)(c) 1995 Act

5.6

An exclusion order can last for a maximum of six months. When the sheriff initially grants the order, it will probably be as an interim order, whether notice has been given or not. An interim order is as good as a full order, unless it has been granted on an emergency basis. In that case, there must be another hearing within three days, after notice to the "named person". Conditions and powers of arrest may be attached to an exclusion order or interim exclusion order after notice.

ss. 79, 77, 78 1995 Act; r.3.36 AS 1997

5.7

When an application is made for an exclusion order, the sheriff may grant a child protection order instead of the exclusion order if satisfied that the conditions for a child protection order are met.

s.76(8) 1995 Act, as amended by Schedule 5, para 2(9) 2011 Act

10

Fostering and kinship care

This chapter briefly outlines the law about fostering, including the different types of fostering, and kinship care.

1 Types of fostering

There are basically two types of fostering:

- public fostering, governed by the 1995 Act and the LAC Regs 2009; and
- private fostering, governed by the 1984 Act and the 1985 Regs.

1995 Act; LAC Regs 2009; 1984 Act; 1985 Regs

1.1

The 2010 Act lists fostering as one of the care services that must be registered and inspected. Schedule 12, paragraph 9 sets out what makes up fostering services and paragraph 10 states how they may be described.

- The "Scottish public fostering service" is the service mentioned in paragraph 9(a) and (b). This is a local authority's own direct service provision under s.26(1) of the 1995 Act *and* their arrangements with voluntary organisations, otherwise called registered fostering services (RFS). Both of these services are for children "looked after" by authorities in terms of the 1995 Act.
- The "Scottish private fostering service" is that mentioned in paragraph 9(c) and the range of duties local authorities have under the 1984 Act.

ss.59 and 83 and Schedule 12, paras 9 and 10 2010 Act; 1995 Act; 1984 Act

1.2

The Care Inspectorate gathers statistics in annual returns from registered services but there can be challenges in achieving accuracy.

There is confusion about the differences between the two types of fostering, and particularly about how private fostering works.

Not all private foster carers are aware of their responsibility to notify the local authority of arrangements or the local authority does not recognise them as private fostering arrangements. They are not facilitated by the local authority or a registered service so it is likely that there are more private fostering arrangements in place than are taking place.

1.3

Both fostering services are regulated by the 2010 Act. From 1 April 2004, all public fostering services run by local authorities and voluntary organisations had to be registered with and inspected by the Care Commission. In addition, local authorities' private fostering services, their duties under the 1984 Act and 1985 Regs, had to be registered with and inspected by the Care Commission from that date. These requirements are contained in the 2010 Act and the services have been registered with and inspected by the Care Inspectorate from 1 April 2011.

ss.59 and 83 and Schedule 12, paras 9 and 10 2010 Act

2 Public fostering

2.1

Public fostering is where children are looked after by local authorities and placed in family homes with approved foster carers. The children may be looked after in one of a variety of ways. All fostered children are looked after and are therefore the responsibility of the local authority duties set out in the LAC Regulations 2009. The same regulations relate to all aspects of foster carers' assessment, approval and placement of children in foster care.

ss.25 and 26 1995 Act; LAC Regs 2009, including Regs 17–33 and Regs 48 and 49 and Schedules 3, 4 and 6

2.2

The LAC Regs 2009 deal with the following:

- the establishment of fostering panels;
- the assessment and approval of foster carers;
- reviews of foster carers' approval;
- placements in foster care and notifications of them;
- short-term placements – respite care;
- case records for foster carers;
- fostering allowances; and
- arrangements between local authorities and RFSs.

There are also Schedules that set out the information which should be obtained on the prospective foster carers when they are assessed; matters to be covered in individual Foster Carer Agreements, i.e. contracts between foster carers and the authority or RFS which approved them; and matters relating to individual Foster Placement Agreements about each child placed.

LAC Regs 2009

2.3

All foster carers must be assessed and approved by local authorities or RFSs. Local authorities can place children with carers approved by other authorities or by RFSs. All local authorities and RFSs have a fostering panel. These panels make recommendations on the approval, etc, of carers.[32]

LAC Regs 2009, Regs 17–20 and Reg 48

2.4

Public foster carers do not acquire parental responsibilities and rights (PRRs) simply through fostering a child. Carers have general duties and rights in relation to the children in their care under s.5 of the 1995 Act, and may be able to consent to medical treatment. Foster carers who look after children who are subject to compulsory supervision orders and interim compulsory supervision orders may be "deemed" relevant persons for the purposes of the hearing system, depending on whether they satisfy the test of having or recently having had significant involvement in the child's upbringing. Foster carers who look after children under permanence orders or permanence orders with authority to adopt may have some PRRs for them, depending on the terms of the individual order and may hold some ancillary provisions in respect of the child.

s.5 1995 Act; s.81 2011 Act; ss.80 and 82 2007 Act

2.5

Registered fostering services (RFSs) assess and approve foster carers in the same way as local authorities. A RFS must be a voluntary organisation, which is defined as 'a body, other than a public or local authority, the activities of which are not carried on for profit'. Before a RFS may provide foster carers to a local authority, it must make formal arrangements with the authority, under Reg 48 of the LAC Regs 2009, as amended.

ss.59(3) and 105(1) 2010 Act; LAC Regs 2009, Reg 2 as amended for the 2010 Act, Reg 48 as amended and Schedule 7

2.6

32 *Effective Adoption and Fostering Panels in Scotland* (Morrison, 2021, CoramBAAF)

Local authorities and RFSs must take account of the Fostering Standards and are inspected against them.

s.50 2010 Act

3 Private fostering

In a private fostering arrangement there will be no statutory order in place, children's services involvement or registered fostering agency involved in placing the child with the other person, i.e. the child is not defined as a "looked after child".

3.1

Private fostering is care provided on a private basis by arrangement between parents and someone who is *not* a close relative. As explained above, it is to be distinguished from public foster care arranged by the local authority.

3.2

Separate legislation covers private fostering arrangements. Arrangements are private fostering ones when:

- the arrangements are made by someone who has parental responsibilities and rights for the child;
- the child is placed with someone who is not a close relative or guardian;
- the child is under the compulsory school leaving age; and
- the care arrangements are for 28 days or more.

ss.1, 2 1984 Act

3.3

A "relative" is defined in the 1984 Act as grandparents, brothers and sisters, uncles and aunts, whether full or half blood or by affinity (relationship through marriage or civil partnership). So, if more distant relatives care for a child for more than 28 days, that is a private fostering arrangement.

s.21 1984 Act

3.4

Where such private arrangements are made, the parent and carer must notify the local authority not less than two weeks before the arrangement starts, unless it is an emergency. In the case of an emergency, notification must be made within one week.

ss.4, 5 1984 Act; 1985 Regs

3.5

When the local authority is notified, it has a duty to be satisfied about the wellbeing of the child and give such advice as to the care and maintenance of the child as may appear to be necessary. The statutory responsibility for securing and monitoring the welfare of any child in a private fostering arrangement lies with the local authority. It is the duty of every local authority to secure the welfare of children within their area who are privately fostered. The child must be visited within one week of the placement and on a regular basis thereafter. The authority may prohibit such private arrangements, or impose conditions on the arrangements.

ss.3, 9, 10 1984 Act; 1985 Regs

3.6

Some people may be disqualified from being private foster carers, including those convicted of certain criminal offences and/or those who have been refused registration or removed from registration as childminders.

s.7 1984 Act

3.7

Private foster carers who are caring for children do not have PRRs. They have general rights of control because they are acting in the place of parents. They must return the child to their parents on request unless they have obtained some other authority to keep the child.

3.8

Private foster carers have a general obligation to safeguard and protect the child's welfare and the right to consent to medical treatment in certain circumstances.

s.5 1995 Act

3.9

Although local authorities' private fostering services must be registered with and inspected by the Care Inspectorate, there are no National Care Standards for private fostering. However, Scottish Government guidance was issued in 2013.

Be Safe, be Sure: Private fostering in Scotland practice guidance for local authority children's services[33]

4 Kinship care

4.1 Looked after children

The term "kinship care" covers a wide variety of arrangements under which children are cared for by family members or friends. However, the LAC Regs 2009 deal with specific kinship care arrangements for looked after children. Local authorities may formally approve kinship carers for looked after children. Unlike foster carers, kinship carers are approved to care for specific looked after

33 00439291.pdf (www.gov.scot)

children, and they may be approved only by local authorities. Kinship carers must be related to the child they are caring for or be people who are 'known to the child or with whom the child has a pre-existing relationship' (Reg 10(2)).

Particularly Regs 10–16, 33 and Schedules 3–5 LAC Regs 2009

4.2

Children living with approved kinship carers are looked after in one of a variety of ways. The arrangements for these children, as for all looked after children, are covered by the local authority duties in the LAC Regs 2009. The same regulations also cover all aspects of kinship carers' assessment, approval, etc, and placement with kinship carers.

ss.25, 26 1995 Act; s.80 2007 Act; ss.91, 119 2011 Act; Regs 10–16, 33 and Schedules 3–5 LAC Regs 2009

4.3

For kinship carers, the LAC Regs 2009 cover:

- the assessment and approval of kinship carers;
- placements in kinship care and notifications of them;
- short-term placements – respite care;
- case records for kinship carers; and
- kinship care allowances.

There are also Schedules that set out the information to be obtained about prospective kinship carers when they are assessed; matters to be covered in individual Kinship Carer Agreements, i.e. contracts between kinship carers and the local authority that approved them; and matters to be covered in individual Kinship Placement Agreements, about each child placed.

LAC Regs 2009

5 Placing a looked after child with kinship carers

5.1

A looked after child may be placed with kinship carers where:

- carers are assessed and approved as suitable to care for the child;
- the placement is in the child's best interests;
- carers have entered into a written agreement with the local authority on specified matters and obligations.

A written case record must be compiled and retained about the carer, members of their household and their family.

5.2

Short-term placements with kinship carers can be treated as one placement in terms of assessment providing:

- all the placements occur within 12 months;
- any one placement does not last longer than four weeks;
- the total duration of the placements is no more than 120 days.

5.3

As soon as is reasonably practicable after placement, the local authority must notify:

- the local authority and health board where the carers live;
- each parent of the child and anyone with PRRs for the child;
  except
  - where that person already has a copy of the Child's Plan
  - where the local authority considers that notifying them would not be

in the child's best interests

- where a permanence order or children's hearing order has a non-disclosure measure in respect of that person.

Looked After Children (Scotland) Regulations 2009 Part V Kinship Care

5.4

There is no requirement for local authorities to have kinship care panels, but some local authorities have established these. Other local authorities use their fostering or other panels to consider kinship carer approvals.

5.5

Kinship carers do not acquire PRRs simply because of the placements. Carers have general duties and rights in relation to the children in their care under s.5 of the 1995 Act, and may be able to consent to medical treatment. Kinship carers who look after children who are subject to compulsory supervision orders and interim compulsory supervision orders may be "deemed" relevant persons for the purposes of the hearing system. Kinship carers who look after children under permanence orders or permanence orders with authority to adopt may have some PRRs for them, depending on the terms of the individual order.

s.5 1995 Act; s.81 2011 Act; ss.80 and 82 2007 Act

6 Non-looked after children

6.1 Kinship care order (KCO)

The Children and Young People (Scotland) Act 2014 referred to kinship care orders. Prior to this, they were known as residence or s.11 orders.

s.11 Children (Scotland) Act; Part 13 Children and Young People (Scotland) Act 2014

It is a private law arrangement that allows a court to make an order about PRRs, guardianship or a child's property. An application can be made only by a person who:

- is related to the child;
- is a friend/acquaintance of a person who is related to the child;
- has a relationship or connection to the child.

s.72(2) 2014 Act

7 Child's views

Before deciding to make an order or not under s.11, the court must:

- Give the child an opportunity to express their views in the manner that the child prefers, or one that is suitable for the child if they have not indicated a preference or where it would be unreasonable to accommodate the child's preference.
- Have regard to any views expressed by the child, taking into account the child's age and maturity. The child is to be presumed to be capable of forming a view unless the contrary is shown.
- Ensure that the decision is explained to the child in a way that the child can understand.

ss.1 and 20 2020 Act

8 Effect of the kinship care order

8.1

A kinship care order can ensure a more stable care arrangement for the child. The kinship carer will acquire some or all the PRRs under a kinship care order; however, the child's parents may retain some of the PRRs that they held before the kinship care order was granted. Having PRRs will allow the carer to make a range of decisions in relation to a child's day to day life – such as:

- consenting to a child's medical procedures;
- obtaining a passport for the child;
- being responsible for their property;
- making decisions about the child's education.

8.2

Once a kinship care order has been granted, the child may no longer be "looked after" by a local authority and there may be no further social work involvement with them. The child will not automatically be entitled to continuing care and after care when they reach the age of 16 if they are no longer a looked after child. A kinship care order may continue until the child is 16 and in exceptional cases, until they are 18. The local authority must provide information and advice to those seeking, holding or subject to a kinship care order.

9 Support for kinship carers

9.1

Local authorities have a duty to ensure that assistance is made available to kinship carers and the children in their care who are applying for or have a kinship care order. This includes but is not exclusive to the local authority providing advice, counselling, information, financial support or subsidising a provision of service to a person holding a kinship care order. A local authority must provide kinship care assistance in such a way as to safeguard, support and promote the wellbeing of an eligible child and describes the types of kinship care assistance that are to be made available to different groups of people.

Part 13 2014 Act; Kinship Care Assistance (Scotland) Order 2016

9.2

The aim of the additional funding is to ensure local parity of allowances between kinship and foster carers. Kinship carers covered by this agreement should receive an allowance at a minimum of the same rate as foster carers in their local authority area. The provision of these allowances was designed to ensure that, regardless of the care setting, a looked after child or a child at risk within a locality, would receive the same financial support. Foster care fees, however, would not be paid to kinship carers.

9.3

This agreement will not apply to all kinship carers. It applies to:

- all kinship carers where the child has a looked after status; and
- some kinship carers, where the child is not a looked after child but is subject to a s.11 order (to be known as a kinship care order), and is or was:
  - previously looked after;
  - placed with involvement from the local authority; or
  - at risk of becoming looked after.

10 Eligibility for support

10.1

The Act specifies which kinship carers and children will be entitled to assistance. This will depend on whether or not the child in their care is an "eligible child", namely, a child who the local authority considers:

- to be at risk of becoming looked after; or
- to fall within such other description as the Scottish Ministers may by order specify.

s.71(5) 2014 Act; Local Authority's Duty to Support

10.2

If the child is deemed to be an "eligible child", and living within the area, the local authority must provide support or arrange assistance to:

- a carer who has or is considering applying for a kinship care order for a child under the age of 16;
- a child who is under the age of 16;
- a child who is 16 or older and just before turning 16 was subject to a kinship care order;
- a guardian under s.7 1995 Act of an eligible child who is under 16.

s.71(3) 2014 Act

11 National guidance

In 2016, the Scottish Government issued guidance to explain the provisions of kinship care orders and kinship care assistance as enacted in the 2014 Act[34] and the 2016 Order.[35] This was refreshed in 2024[36] and a new National Assessment Framework published that year.[37]

34 https://www.legislation.gov.uk/asp/2014/8/contents/enacted

35 https://www.legislation.gov.uk/ssi/2016/153/contents/made

36 Supporting documents: Kinship Care: Children and Young People (Scotland) Act 2014 - part 13 (updated guidance 2024), https://tinyurl.com/bdh2sa22

37 Kinship care: Assessment framework (2024), https://tinyurl.com/mr3mek7x

11

The children's hearing system

1 The system

The children's hearing system was established in 1971 and is a uniquely Scottish approach providing care and justice to children who require the intervention and support of agencies to safeguard their welfare. The most relevant legislation under which a children's hearing operates is the Children's Hearings (Scotland) Act 2011 and The Children's Hearings (Scotland) Act 2011 (Rules of Procedure in Children's Hearings) Rules 2013 – the latter usually just referred to as "The 2013 Rules". These take account of the obligation of consistency and compatibility with the decisions of the ECHR and recognise the importance of children's rights under the United Nations Convention on the Rights of the Child (UNCRC).

2 Ethos of the system

2.1

The distinguishing feature of the system is the focus on the needs of the child, whether the child has committed an offence or they are at risk due to neglect, abuse or because of their own behaviour. The child is spared the formality and adversarial nature of a court setting, instead attending a children's hearing on referral by the Children's Reporter, where their welfare needs are the focus of discussion and decision making. Since its introduction, children charged with a crime are dealt with in the adult system only in rare and particular circumstances. There is no punitive aspect to the system – simply a recognition that the child may require guidance, treatment, control or protection to enable them to fulfil their potential. An order by the children's hearing may be issued to support the child in this.

Principles of the Children's Hearings System

2.2

The decision making in the children's hearings is underpinned by three overarching principles.

These are:

1. The need to safeguard and promote the welfare of the child throughout their childhood is the paramount consideration. (The exception being when the child's welfare becomes the primary, rather than paramount consideration for the purpose of protecting members of the public from serious harm (whether physical or not)).
2. A legal order should only be made where it would be better for the child than no order being made.

ss.25–28 2011 Act

3. In children's hearings proceedings, the hearing or court must have regard to any views expressed by the child, taking account of the child's age and maturity, except where they are satisfied that the child is not capable of forming a view or the child's location is unknown.

   However, the child is presumed to be capable of forming a view unless the contrary is shown.

The child must be given the opportunity to express their views in a manner they prefer or one that is suitable to them if they have not indicated a preference or where it would be unreasonable to accommodate that preference in the circumstances.

s.3 Children (Scotland) Act 2020

3 Development of the system

3.1

The hearing system moves with the times and takes account of policy developments to ensure that the hearings reflect improved understanding of how best to meet the needs of the child. Getting it Right for Every Child (GIRFEC), now embedded in legislation under the Children and Young People (Scotland) Act 2014, places an emphasis on early intervention, collaborative working among agencies and diverting young people away from offending.

Proposed changes and improvements to the system were outlined in a comprehensive report published in May 2023 – The **Hearings for Children Redesign Report**.[38] Some of these recommendations are likely to be implemented in 2025 through the Children (Care, Care Experience and Services Planning) Bill.

3.2

With the passing of the Act, anyone under the age of 18 (including those involved in criminality) will be referred to the Children's Reporter for any ground of referral, once this part of the forthcoming legislation is operational.

The threshold is lowered for the use of Movement Restriction Conditions which may be invoked to protect the child themselves or any possible victim. Within the hearing system, children may be detained in secure accommodation, rather than being placed in young offenders institutions, where courts dealing with their offending may have detained them.

Currently, relevant persons have wide-ranging and specific rights; whether these will apply to children over the age of 16 is uncertain, particularly taking account of the child's right to privacy.

Children (Care and Justice) (Scotland) Act 2020

4 Permanence considerations

38 https://thepromise.scot/resources/2023/hearings-for-children-the-redesign-report.pdf

The impetus to achieve safety, security and stability in the child's life as early as is practicable has also meant that consideration is given to planning for permanence. Permanence might take place at home with or without support from agencies; or with the child living with family members or carers; or living in a residential establishment; or the child being placed with long-term foster carers or adoptive parents. However, avoiding drift, uncertainty and delay in a child's life is a significant motivator in decision making. Hearings are increasingly required to make decisions about children where rehabilitation with birth parents is assessed as not being viable. The local authority is required to plan for the child's permanence and to present these plans to the hearing. Panel members are trained to recognise the role they have to play in ensuring that every child reaches permanence.

5 Patterns of referral

The number of referrals to the Reporter has steadily reduced over the years, which reflects the diversion and intervention of agencies in working with families to overcome difficulties without need for formal measures to be put in place at a children's hearing. This is in line with the proportionate minimum intervention approach adopted by agencies. Historically, the majority of referrals involved the child's offending behaviour; now the majority relate to concerns for the child's care and protection in its wider sense with a more trauma-informed approach, recognising the life-long impact on children of Adverse Childhood Experiences (ACEs).

6 Significant people in the hearing system

6.1 Reporter to the children's panel

The reporter's service operates on a national basis as the Scottish Children's Reporter Administration (SCRA) and the 2011 Act provides the legislative basis or SCRA. There is a Principal Reporter and SCRA has nine localities, supported by a head office, based in Stirling.

The 2013 Rules extensively set out the reporter's duties, adding specification to the primary legislation.

The reporter's main role is to receive referrals for children who may require compulsory measures of supervision which they have a legal duty to investigate.

They act in some ways like a clerk to a hearing, but they have many other duties throughout the wider system. They will request reports from agencies and make a decision as to whether or not to refer a child to a children's hearing.

Where the reporter decides to arrange a hearing, they will draw up a Statement of Grounds to be put to the child and relevant persons at the hearing.

The reporter is responsible for providing premises for the hearings to take place.

Before the hearing, they will be responsible for the administration of the hearing – sending notifications and papers to the child, family and panel members, requesting reports and also arranging the hearing.

During the hearing, they will be responsible for keeping a record of the proceedings and supporting fair process. Although they may provide a view on the law or procedure, they will not take part in the discussion in the hearing and are not involved in the decision-making.

After the hearing, they will notify the hearing's decision to the family, child and agencies.

Where a child or young person is referred to a children's hearing and the Statement of Grounds is not accepted, or the child or young person does not understand due to their age or ability, the hearing can direct the reporter to make an application to the sheriff to decide whether the grounds are established. The reporter will conduct the case in court, including leading evidence before the sheriff. If the sheriff is satisfied that the grounds are correct, the Reporter will arrange another hearing to decide whether the child or young person requires compulsory measures.

Where decisions are appealed to the court, the reporter will promote the hearing's decision where this is supportable.

ss.14–24 and Schedule 3 2011 Act

6.2 Panel members

Each hearing is an independent legal tribunal made up of three trained lay persons who make the decisions, called children's panel members. Children's Hearings Scotland (CHS) was set up in 2013 to manage, recruit, offer national training and support panel members throughout Scotland. The National Convener of Children's Hearings Scotland is responsible for this and they and their office are helped by Area Support Teams, which operate on a local basis. CHS also deals with any complaints about panel members and promotes an effective working partnership with key stakeholders in the local area.

Panel members are observed and assessed in hearings by a Panel Practice Adviser – a member of the Area Support Team who supports and promotes best practice and performance.

There are approximately 2,500 children's hearing panel members in Scotland. Before becoming panel members, they undertake extensive training in the legal processes, child development and their own role within the hearing system. They require further training before being able to chair hearings and they receive ongoing training throughout their time as panel members. This includes attendance at mandatory training sessions and local and national information, training and skills development sessions throughout the year.

Panel members are recruited for a three-year period, after which they are eligible for re-appointment.

Panel members are drawn from the local community where they are sitting on hearings. Because they either live or work in that local authority area, they will be familiar with where the child lives and the particular challenges and issues within the community. Panel members will be at least 18 years of age, although there is no upper age limit, and they come from a variety of backgrounds.

Panel members sit on hearings on a rota basis. Three panel members sit on each hearing and there must be a mix of men and women. Panel members will generally sit on one–four hearings each month.

2011 Act, ss.1–13 and Schedules 1, 2 and 4; 2013 Rules Part 2

6.3 Safeguarders

There are regulations with detailed provisions about safeguarders. There is a national Safeguarders Panel for Scotland, and its management and operation is carried out by the Scottish charity Children First. It supports and promotes safeguarders' best practice. There is some information on their website – see Further Reading.

ss.30–34 and s.82 2011 Act; Regs 9, 31, 56, 57 2013 Rules

The function of a safeguarder is essentially to provide an "independent" view of the child's case. They should look at the case from the perspective of the child's best interests. A safeguarder may be appointed by a children's hearing or pre-hearing panel in any case, or by a sheriff who is dealing with grounds for referral, appeals or reviews of grounds established.

Every children's hearing must consider the appointment of a safeguarder and provide reasons for their appointment or the decision not to appoint one. Legislation does not give possible reasons for the safeguarder's appointment other than the general one in relation to safeguarding the child's interests. In practice, safeguarders are often appointed for a variety of reasons, including where there is conflicting information and the hearing wants clarity of a situation or where the hearing wants to receive the child's views.

The safeguarder receives all papers available to the panel members and has a right to attend hearings and court proceedings in relation to that appointment. They will interview professionals involved in the case, relevant persons, the child and anyone else whom they believe has information that would help them in their investigation. They will provide a report and a recommendation to the hearing and this will be available to the Reporter, relevant persons and the child. The social worker has no right to receive this report, although some safeguarders recognise the usefulness in making this available to the worker.

Once a substantive decision is made, the safeguarder's appointment comes to an end, although they do have the right to appeal the hearing's decision.

CH Rules 2013, rr.22 and 26 and r.88; 2.154, s.163 and s.34 2011 Act

6.4 Relevant persons

Once a child has been referred to the reporter, their relationships with the adults in their life becomes of significant legal importance because it determines who has a right to be involved in the proceedings.

In the 1995 Act, the term used for an adult with a range of rights in the hearing system was "relevant person" (not "parent"). The same term is used in the 2011 Act, and a person who is a relevant person has much the same rights as under the 1995 Act.

Under the 2011 Act, there are two types of relevant persons: "automatic" ones and "deemed" ones. They all have the same rights and duties, but the ways in which they are relevant persons are different.

6.5 Automatic relevant persons

"Automatic" relevant persons are people who have the status automatically, because of the statutory definition. Their status remains for all hearings and cannot be removed. Section 200 of the 2011 Act, as amended, says that the following people are relevant persons, "automatically":

1. *a parent or guardian with parental responsibilities and/or rights under Part I of the 1995 Act, i.e. under Scots Law;*
2. *a parent with no parental responsibilities or rights (as long as they did not have them previously and then lost them through a court order);*
3. *a person with parental responsibilities and/or rights from an order made under the 1995 Act, s.11, and which gave some or all of these and/or residence, but excluding someone who only has a contact or specific issue order;*
4. *a parent with parental responsibility under the Children Act 1989 or Adoption and Children Act 2002, i.e. under English and Welsh law;*

5. *a person with parental responsibilities under the Children (Northern Ireland) Order 1995, i.e. under Northern Irish law; and*

6. *a person with parental responsibilities and/or rights under a permanence order.*

s.200 2011 Act, as added to by the Children's Hearings (Scotland) Act 2011 (Review of Contact Directions and Definition of Relevant Person) Order 2013, SSI 2013/193, para 3

6.6 *Deemed relevant persons*

Other people may be deemed relevant persons by children's hearings. As with automatic relevant person status, this is a factual test and not based on what is in the child's best interests. The child, existing relevant persons and people who wish to be relevant persons may all ask for a hearing to have someone or themselves deemed as relevant persons. The Reporter may also ask for this. The hearing makes a decision at a pre-hearing panel or a full hearing. Panel members must deem someone a relevant person if they think 'that the individual has (or has recently had) a significant involvement in the upbringing of the child'. Once someone is deemed a relevant person, they retain that status, unless and until a future review hearing considers that they 'may no longer have (nor recently have had) a significant involvement in the upbringing of the child'. There are rights of appeal against a decision that someone is or is not a relevant person. Such an appeal must be made within seven days and then heard within three days.

ss.79–81, s.142, and ss.160 and 164 2011 Act

A court ruling in 2013[39] provided some clarification about what considerations should be taken into account when deciding if someone has or has recently had significant involvement in the upbringing of the child. It recognised that decisions may involve sensitive and complex issues and that each child's relationship with the adult must be considered individually. A day-to-day involvement in the child's care can be important but will not in itself mean that

39 MT and AG against Anne Gerry (locality reporter) [2014] CSIH 108

someone is deemed to be a relevant person. Other factors to be considered are:

- Where the child is sufficiently mature, their view should be sought as to the significance of the relationship with the adult.
- The length of time that a person has been involved in the child's life.
- Whether the carer fulfils a parenting role in terms of making key decisions, for example, about education and medical treatment.
- A detailed consideration should be given to the terms and implementation of each written fostering agreement. This helps to clarify what the expectations are both of and by the carers in terms of their long-term commitment to the child's upbringing. A child could have been with carers for months or even years with no prospect of the carer continuing to care for the child and major decisions being made by the local authority and the child's parents. Alternatively, a child may have been with carers for only a few months but placed there in anticipation of the carers having a responsibility in the child's upbringing into the future.
- The presence of a blood tie with the child should be taken into account. Where, for example, a grandparent does not actually live with the child but has regular, even overnight contact with them and contributes to decision-making about important matters in their life, this will be of significance.
- Whether the prospective relevant person lives in the same house as the child is important. If they do not, then the level and quality of contact between that person and the child should be explored.

6.7 Rights of relevant person

A relevant person has a range of rights, including the right to:

- be sent notification of each hearing;
- be sent all the papers, reports, etc;
- attend the child's hearing, and has a duty as well, unless the hearing is

satisfied that it would be unreasonable for them to attend;

- bring a representative and a legal representative to each hearing;
- be asked if s.67 grounds are accepted or not;
- receive written notification of the decision of each hearing;
- attend any proof hearing and be represented;
- appeal against decisions; and
- ask for a review any time after three months from the previous decision.

s.74, s.78(1)(c), s.90, s.104, s.106, s.132, s.154, ss.158–160 and ss.162 and 163 2011 Act; CH Rules 2013

7 Process on referral

7.1 Referral to the reporter

Currently a child may be referred to the reporter up until they are 16 or where already subject to a compulsory supervision order, up until the age of 18. However, once a child is subject to a compulsory supervision order, they may stay in the system until 18. Any child under 16 may be referred to the reporter; and the reporter may refer a child not already subject to a compulsory supervision order to a hearing after their 16th birthday, provided that the referral was received before that date. In practice, the referral of a child to the reporter near their 16th birthday may be of little assistance to them if they are not already subject to a compulsory supervision order.

Children (Care and Justice) (Scotland) Act

7.2

Anyone *may* provide information or refer a child to the reporter where the person considers:

(a) *that the child is in need of protection, guidance, treatment or control, and*

(b) *that it might be necessary for a compulsory supervision order to be made in relation to the child.*

When the local authority considers that this applies to a child, it has a *duty* to enquire into the child's circumstances and to refer to the reporter. The police also have a *duty* to refer and any other person *may* do so. The bulk of referrals come from the local authority, usually social work and other referrals from education departments, the police and health services.

ss.60–64 2011 Act

7.3 Grounds for referral

Anyone making a referral will probably think about the possible grounds of referral but the decisions about whether there are grounds, and if so, which ones apply, are for the reporter. This means that if any person or body is concerned about a child, they can refer whether or not they are certain about grounds for referral.

7.4

The grounds for referring a child to a hearing are in s.67 of the 2011 Act and are called 'section 67 grounds'. These are that:

(a) *the child is likely to suffer unnecessarily, or is likely to have his or her health or development seriously impaired, due to a lack of parental care;*

(b) *the child has had committed against him or her any of the offences listed in Schedule 1 to the Criminal Procedure (Scotland) Act 1995;*

(c) *the child has, or is likely to have, a close connection with a person who has committed a Schedule 1 offence;*

(d) *the child is, or is likely to become, a member of the same household as a child in respect of whom a Schedule 1 offence has been committed;*

(e) *the child is being, or is likely to be, exposed to persons whose conduct is (or has been) such that it is likely that –*

(i) *the child will be abused or harmed, or*

(ii) *the child's health, safety or development will be seriously adversely affected;*

(f) *the child has, or is likely to have, a close connection with a person who has carried out domestic abuse;*

(g) *the child has, or is likely to have, a close connection with a person who has committed an offence under Parts 1, 4 or 5 of the Sexual Offences (Scotland) Act 2009;*

(h) *the child is being provided with accommodation by a local authority under s.25 of the 1995 Act and special measures are needed to support the child;*

(i) *a permanence order is in force in respect of the child and special measures are needed to support the child;*

(j) *the child has committed an offence;*

(k) *the child has misused alcohol;*

(l) *the child has misused a drug (whether or not a controlled drug);*

(m) *the child's conduct has had, or is likely to have, a serious adverse effect on the health, safety or development of the child or another person;*

(n) *the child is beyond the control of a relevant person;*

(o) *the child has failed without reasonable excuse to attend regularly at school;*

(p) *the child –*

(i) *is being, or is likely to be, subjected to physical, emotional or other pressure to enter into a civil partnership, or*

(ii) *is, or is likely to become, a member of the same household as such a child, (q)* *the child –*

(i) has been, is being or is likely to be forced into a marriage (as in s.1 of the Forced Marriage etc (Protection and Jurisdiction) (Scotland) Act 2011), or

(ii) is, or is likely to become, a member of the same household as such a child.

s.67(2) 2011 Act, as amended by s.13 FM Act 2011

Where the grounds refer to a child having 'a close connection with a person, it means that the child is member of the same household as the person, or...has significant contact with the person.'

s.67(3) 2011 Act

"Significant contact" should be interpreted in a way that considers the underlying purpose of the ground – to prevent the child being subject to the same behaviour as the person in question already subjected another child. Therefore it should not only relate to the volume of contact, but also the nature of the contact and the whole circumstances relating to the contact, e.g. the nature of the relationship between the child and the person, the nature and purpose of the contact, and the reasons for any temporary suspension of the contact (with no one factor being determinative).[40]

Kearney says:

> *The context here is the protection of the child and it is therefore suggested that where there is a real possibility that the connection would put the child at risk then this would be enough.*[41]

7.5 Reporter's decision-making options

When a child has been referred to the reporter, they must decide whether a ground for referral applies and, if so, whether a compulsory supervision order is

40 SCRA Practice Direction 7

41 Butterworths' Family Law Service (at paragraph C2021)

necessary for the child. The reporter has three options and must decide:

- that a hearing is not required and inform the child's family, etc, of this decision; *or*
- that a hearing is not necessary but that it is appropriate to refer the case to the local authority to provide 'advice, guidance and assistance to the child and the child's family' in terms of the local authority's duties in ss.16–38 of the 1995 Act; *or*
- to arrange a children's hearing because the reporter thinks a compulsory supervision order is "necessary" for the child – in other words, an order seems needed.

ss.66–269 011 Act

7.6

In essence, the reporter's decision to proceed to a hearing is made on the basis that:

- the child needs compulsory measures of supervision, i.e. there is a basis for statutory intervention, looking at the child's welfare; *and*
- there is sufficient evidence to establish one or more of the grounds for referral in s.67 – see above.

s.66 2011 Act

8 Hearings, pre-hearings and emergency hearings

8.1

Hearings may be held for a range of reasons, and may make final or interim decisions. The 2011 Act introduced pre-hearing panels (PHPs) as well. These may deal with whether someone should or should not be deemed a relevant person, whether a child or relevant person may be excused from attending a hearing, whether the full hearing is likely to consider making a secure accommodation authorisation, and other matters in the CH Rules 2013, including non-disclosure of information to any of the parties. When a full hearing is arranged, this could be for a range of matters, including:

- for new s.67 grounds for referral; *or*
- a continuation of an existing case; *or*
- to deal with s.67 grounds established at court; *or*
- to review an existing compulsory supervision order; *or*
- to deal with a child protection emergency; *or*
- to provide advice to a criminal court or about permanence plans.

The 2011 Act and CH Rules 2013 have detailed rules about the preparation for and the running and chairing of hearings and pre-hearing panels.

2011 Act, including ss.79–81; CH Rules 2013

8.2 *Legal notice of a hearing and PHP*

For a full hearing, unless it is an emergency one, a reporter must usually give seven days' notice of the date, time, place, etc, to the child and relevant persons. Where grounds for referral are put, at least seven days' notice of the actual grounds themselves must be given. For a pre-hearing panel, five days' notice should be given if practicable.

CH Rules 2011, including rr.22 and 23, r.27, r.29 and rr.45 and 46

8.3 *Child's rights and duty to attend*

A child has a right and a duty to attend their hearing. A child may be excused from attending if the grounds relate to offences against the child or other children and the child's attendance is not necessary for a fair hearing; or if attendance would put 'the child's physical, mental or moral welfare at risk'; or if the child 'would not be capable of understanding what happens at the hearing' or for the reading of grounds where they are unlikely to understand any explanation, taking account of age and maturity. A child can insist on attending even if excused. The child also has a right to bring a representative to the hearing and to have legal representation if they understand generally what it means to instruct a solicitor.

ss.73 and 78(1)(a) and (b) 2011 Act; CH Rules 2013, r.11; s.2(4A) 1991 Act

8.4 Relevant person's right and duty to attend

Relevant persons have a duty and right to attend a hearing. A hearing may dispense with this duty for all or part of the hearing if satisfied that it would be unreasonable to require them to attend or where unnecessary for the proper consideration of the matter before the hearing.

The relevant person retains the right to attend a hearing even where their duty to attend has been dispensed with.

Panel members may exclude a relevant person and/or representative for any part of the hearing. They can do so if they feel it is necessary to find out the child's views, or if the presence of the person is causing or is likely to cause the child 'significant distress'. Where someone is excluded in this way, the Chair of the hearing must explain 'what has taken place' to them in their absence.

ss.74, 76 and 77 2011 Act

8.5 Non-relevant person's right to attend

Simply because someone is not deemed to be a relevant person does not mean that they cannot attend the hearing; it just means that they do not have a right to attend in the capacity as a relevant person and it is instead at the discretion of the panel/Chair as to whether they attend. Therefore a foster carer who is not deemed to be a relevant person could attend the hearing in their capacity as a person who attends to the child's day-to-day needs, and their input in that capacity will be helpful to the hearing in their discussion and deliberations.

Similarly, for example, a grandparent who is not deemed to be a relevant person may be asked by a parent to attend the hearing as a friend or supporter and in that position have rights to attend and contribute to the hearing.

8.6 *Process in a children's hearing*

Where a reporter has arranged a hearing, they must request a report on the child from the local authority, unless it already exists as part of the initial investigation. Further additional information may be sought from the local authority.

s.69 2011 Act

Where the reporter refers to a children's hearing, before the hearing, the child and every relevant person should be sent all the information and reports prepared for the hearing. These are the same reports that are sent to panel members, and also to any safeguarder who has been appointed. In practice, reports, etc, are not usually sent to very young children.

CH Rules 2013, including r.18

8.7

Panel members consider reports on the child's circumstances and discuss these at the hearing with the child, the child's parents and any other important adults in the child's life – referred to as relevant persons. Also present at the hearing and giving their views and recommendations are professionals such as social workers, teachers and health visitors. The reporter to the children's panel will be present to administer the hearing and to uphold fair process.

The child and relevant persons have a right, and are encouraged, to express their views to help inform the panel members' decision. However, the panel members have sole responsibility for making a decision and the decisions made at a hearing are legally binding. Each panel member makes their decision at the end of the hearing and the majority decision prevails. The chairing member of the hearing will inform all those present of the decision where a substantive decision has been made. The child, relevant persons and safeguarder have the right to appeal that decision to the Sheriff Court. These reasons and the decision will be "written up" after the hearing by the panel members and then sent to the child and relevant persons.

Panel members have to decide if a young person is in need of compulsory measures of supervision. A compulsory supervision order means that the local authority identified as being responsible for implementing the order is obliged to work with the child and family in the terms laid out by the hearing.

8.8

The CH Rules 2013 contain detailed provisions about procedures for many different types of hearings. These are generally similar but vary depending on the purpose and/or outcome of each individual hearing. As indicated, at the hearing the child and any relevant person may each be accompanied by a representative. The Chair must explain the purpose of the hearing and go over any s.67 grounds. They must explain the substance of the reports that the panel members, the relevant person/s and the child have received. After considering the case, the panel members must reach a decision. Before the close of the hearing, the Chair must tell the child and relevant person/s:

- what the decision is;
- the reasons for it; and
- any rights of appeal against the decision.

There are also rules about written notification of the decision. The decision could be to defer making a decision at that hearing.

CH Rules 2013, including rr.6 and 7, r.13, rr.48 and 49, r.58–83, rr.86, 87 and 95

8.9

Generally, hearings, emergency hearings, pre-hearing panels and related court proceedings are conducted in terms of the principles of the 2011 Act – see Chapter 2. This means that panel members and courts (except in evidential hearings) must:

- make the child's welfare their paramount consideration in their decisions;
- seek out and have regard of the child's views; and
- not make an order unless they think it is better to make one than not to do so.

In addition, at every hearing, the Chair must ask the child if the reports 'accurately reflect any views expressed by the child'. This is not required if the Chair thinks it would be inappropriate, taking account of the child's age and maturity.

ss.25–29 and s.121 2011 Act

8.10

Sometimes, a hearing is held in an emergency situation. For example, the child may be the subject of a child protection order, in which case there are strict and complicated timetables within which the reporter (if they think a hearing is necessary) must bring the case to the hearing, and the panel members look at the situation. When a hearing meets on an emergency basis, it is not usually able to make a final decision. It is, however, allowed to issue an interim compulsory supervision order (or interim variation of an existing compulsory supervision order) for the child. An interim compulsory supervision order after a child protection order will usually be for the child to be kept in a place of safety for short periods of time, until final arrangements can be made, further investigation can be carried out and/or matters can be taken to court; however, the child may remain at home under such an order. An interim compulsory supervision order may have other measures as well or instead, depending on the case's circumstances.

ss.45–47, s.69, s.86, ss.92–94, ss.96–100, s.109, s.120 2011 Act; s.67 grounds and court applications

Where a hearing has been arranged to put s.67 grounds, the Chair must explain the grounds to the child and relevant person/s. In order to proceed any further, panel members must be satisfied that the child and relevant person/s:

- understand the grounds; and
- accept them wholly or in part.

s.90 2011 Act

If the grounds for referral are fully understood and accepted by the child and relevant person/s, the hearing may go ahead. If the grounds are understood and accepted in part, the panel members may discharge the parts that are not accepted and proceed on the basis of what has been accepted. If the child and/or relevant person/s understand but do not accept the grounds for referral at all, or not enough to allow the hearing to proceed with an accepted part, the panel members must *either*:

- direct the reporter to make an application to the sheriff; *or*
- discharge the whole referral.

If the child is incapable of understanding or does not understand the grounds for referral, again, the hearing must either direct the reporter to apply to the sheriff or discharge the grounds, even if the relevant person/s has accepted them in full.

s.91–94 and s.96 2011 Act

8.11 Court proceedings

If the grounds for referral are sent to the sheriff, they hear evidence on the disputed facts and make a decision based on the normal rules of evidence. If the grounds are accepted between the referral and the proof hearing, the sheriff may send them back to the hearing without a proof. If the proof goes ahead, the sheriff *either*:

- finds the s.67 grounds established in full or in part, and refers them back to a hearing; *or*
- finds them not established and discharges the whole case.

The reporter conducts the proof in front of the sheriff and the burden or onus of proof is on the reporter. All grounds must be established on the "balance of probabilities" (civil standard), except where the referred child is alleged to have committed a crime, when the standard of proof is "beyond reasonable doubt" (criminal standard). The sheriff's decision is not governed by the welfare principle because it is a straight testing of the factual evidence. The sheriff has no power to make any order about the child's welfare in relation to the grounds. Where the sheriff finds the grounds established, they will remit to the hearing for disposal and may make an interim compulsory supervision order if the child's welfare requires some short-term measure.

ss.100–109 2011 Act

8.12 Disposals by hearings: some orders

When there are accepted or established grounds, and/or there is a review of an existing compulsory supervision order, a hearing has a range of options:

- to discharge grounds on the basis that a compulsory supervision order is not necessary;
- to defer making a decision and continue the hearing for further information and/or investigation;
- to make a compulsory supervision order or continue or vary an existing one;
- to terminate an existing compulsory supervision order if it is no longer necessary, even if there are new grounds for referral.

If a case is continued and the hearing members feel that some form of compulsory measure is needed in the short term, they may make an interim compulsory supervision order if one has not already been made, or continue an existing one. If the hearing is reviewing a compulsory supervision order, it may be continued or varied on an interim basis until the next hearing.

8.13 Looked after status

If a child is made subject to a compulsory supervision order or interim compulsory supervision order, they become a "looked after" child, even if living at home. When an order is made, then compulsory measures of supervision are put in place. This means the local authority has duties in respect of the child.

8.14 Local authority duties

A local authority, as the "Implementation Authority", must carry out the terms of compulsory supervision orders. This includes making sure that: children are living where their orders require; other conditions are being carried out; and they are implementing any duties specifically imposed on them in the orders. If hearings feel that local authorities are not complying with their duty, they may authorise the National Convener to apply to the Sheriff Principal about the breach. The Sheriff Principal may make orders requiring local authorities to perform the duties. These provisions about enforcement of local authority duties replace earlier ones in the ASBA 2004.

ss.144–148 2011 Act

9 Appeals

There are rights of appeal within the hearing system. An appeal may be made against: a final decision about a compulsory supervision order; or a decision about an interim compulsory supervision order or a decision about a medical examination order; or the granting of a warrant to secure the child's attendance at a hearing. An appeal must usually be made within three weeks of the decision, to the sheriff. Certain appeals must be heard and disposed of within three days. These are where the appeal is against the making of: a compulsory supervision order with a secure accommodation authorisation, an interim compulsory supervision order, an interim variation of a compulsory supervision order, a medical examination order, or a warrant to secure the child's attendance.

ss.154–157 2011 Act

When a sheriff is dealing with an appeal against an interim compulsory supervision order, or a medical examination order or a warrant, they must either uphold the decision or terminate or recall the order. When a sheriff is dealing with a decision about a compulsory supervision order, they have a range of options. They may confirm the decision with or without further steps; or continue or vary the order appealed against; or overturn the decision, terminate any order and discharge the child from any further proceedings; or may order that a new children's hearing is arranged; or make an interim compulsory supervision order or interim variation of an existing compulsory supervision order; or grant a warrant to secure attendance.

s.156 2011 Act

9.1

There are further rights of appeal from the sheriff to the Sheriff Appeal Court (Civil) or straight to the Court of Session. This can be against *either* a sheriff's appeal decision *or* against a sheriff's finding that grounds for referral are established or not established. The reporter has a right to appeal at this stage, as well as the child, relevant person/s and the safeguarder. If an appeal is made to the Sheriff Appeal Court (Civil), it is possible to appeal again to the Court of Session, with the leave of the Sheriff Appeal Court (Civil).

s.163 2011 Act

9.2

There are other appeal provisions in the 2011 Act. Appeals may be made to the sheriff against decisions about: whether someone should or should not be deemed a relevant person; contact rights for someone who is not a relevant person; and implementation or not of a secure accommodation authorisation. Further appeals may be made to the Sheriff Appeal Court (Civil) and/or the Court of Session. There is also a right to review when a local authority wishes to challenge the fact that it has been named as the implementation authority in a compulsory supervision order, interim compulsory supervision order or medical examination order. After the sheriff has reviewed the matter, there may be an appeal to the Sheriff Appeal Court (Civil), whose decision is final.

ss.160–162 and ss.164–167 2011 Act

10 Reviews

It is and always has been an essential part of the hearing system that no order may last for more than one year without being reviewed. If a supervision requirement is not reviewed within a year, it automatically falls.

s.83(7) 2011 Act

The 2011 Act contains a wide range of possible reviews, including some new ones. Children, relevant persons, the local authority, and hearing members may request reviews, and the reporter has duties to arrange others. The main reviews are where:

- the local authority considers a review is necessary;
- the local authority is planning permanent arrangements for the child (permanence order, permanence order with authority to adopt, or adoption) or an adoption application is proposed;
- the child wishes a review (provided the compulsory supervision order was made, continued or varied more than three months before);
- a relevant person wishes a review (provided the compulsory supervision order was made or varied more than three months before);
- hearing members wish the compulsory supervision order reviewed; and
- the compulsory supervision order will expire in less than three months, in which case the reporter arranges an "annual review".

There are also reviews of secure accommodation authorisations, emergency transfers, movement restriction conditions; and of contact directions. If there is a full review hearing, it may also consider whether a deemed relevant person should continue to be deemed.

s.125 and 126, ss.129–136, ss.142 and 143 2011 Act

10.1

There is also an automatic review when the reporter puts new grounds for referral to a child who is already subject to a compulsory supervision order.

s.97, and s.91 as modified by s.97 2011 Act

10.2

The need for there to be a review when the local authority is planning for permanence means that hearing members must discuss plans for long-term care and adoption and give their opinion on them.

s.131(2)(c)–(e) and s.141 2011 Act

12

Permanence orders

This chapter deals with permanence orders (POs), and permanence orders with authority to adopt (POAs).

1 Introduction

1.1

Permanence orders and permanence orders with authority to adopt are orders designed as options for children who are not able to live at home. They give local authorities some or possibly all PRRs. They may also give some PRRs to carers such as foster or kinship carers; and they take some or possibly all PRRs away from parents. They were introduced by the 2007 Act and the background and theory are set out in Chapter 5 of the 2005 APRG Phase II Report. They are designed to be as flexible as possible, different for each child, to meet their individual needs. All children who are the subject of permanence orders or permanence orders with authority to adopt are looked after by the local authority; and all orders last until the child is 18, unless they are revoked, or the child is adopted. The right to regulate the child's residence ceases when they reach the age of 16.

APRG Report, 2005, Chapter 5; 2007 Act, particularly ss.80–104; s.17(6) as amended 1995 Act

1.2

A permanence order may be a "destination" one (usually a permanence order) *or* the route to adoption (usually but not always a permanence order with authority to adopt). However, if adoption is the plan for a child, it is not essential to seek a permanence order with authority to adopt first. Only a local authority may apply for a permanence order or permanence order with authority to adopt, although parents and others have the right to be parties to all court proceedings. Every order gives the local authority at least one parental responsibility and one right and may give them other PRRs. However, the flexibility arises from the fact that the parents may keep some PRRs, as appropriate in each case, and/or other people, such as foster or kinship carers, may be given some PRRs, again as appropriate in each case.

2 Parts of the permanence order

A permanence order may have up to three parts:

- the mandatory provision, the essential part of the order;
- ancillary provisions, not essential but every order should have some; and
- authority for adoption, but only if adoption is the plan for the child.

ss.80–82 2007 Act

3 Mandatory provision

Every permanence order and permanence order with authority to adopt has a mandatory provision and there cannot be an order unless this is part of it. The mandatory provision is given to the local authority that applied for the order and is the heart or kernel of a permanence order. It has two parts: the parental responsibility to provide the child with guidance; and the parental right to regulate the child's residence, that is, where the child lives. Also, as an automatic part of the order, the parents'/guardians' parental right to control residence is removed.

ss.80, 81 and 87 2007 Act, with reference to ss.1 and 2 1995 Act

4 Ancillary provisions

4.1

If a permanence order is granted with just the mandatory provision, no other PRRs are automatically given to the local authority or removed from the parents. If the applicant local authority wants more PRRs, and wants foster or kinship carers to acquire PRRs, and/or wants some or all of the parents' other PRRs to be removed, it needs to ask the court to do this specifically, as part of the ancillary provisions. It is not essential for a permanence order to have any ancillary provisions. However, if there are no ancillary provisions, it will be difficult to make the permanence order work well for the benefit of the child; and it will not be possible to vary the order in the future.

ss.80, 82 and 92 2007 Act

4.2

Ancillary provisions are about PRRs and other matters to do with the child's welfare. They are the key to an order and what gives it the flexibility needed to suit each child and their circumstances. It is the court that decides what provisions to give and to whom, and what PRRs to take away and from whom. This is done by including ancillary provisions in the order. The local authority applying for an order should plan for and seek the best, most flexible combination of responsibilities, rights, etc, for each child. There should be careful assessment and planning, involving social work and legal practitioners, and others as well.

ss.80 and 82 2007 Act

4.3

There are a wide range of possible ancillary provisions and a wide range of options for the court. The court may:

- give one or more parental responsibilities and/or rights to the local authority; and/or
- give one or more parental responsibilities and/or rights to other people;

and/or

- take away one or more parental responsibilities and/or rights from the parents; and/or
- provide for contact arrangements for the child, and not just with the parents; and/or
- provide for any other orders about PRRs and anything else affecting the child's welfare.

5 Authority for adoption

This is the third possible part of a permanence order, and if it is granted, the order is referred to as a permanence order with authority to adopt. Unlike mandatory and ancillary provisions, many permanence orders do not have this authority, as it is not appropriate unless adoption is the plan for the child. When authority for adoption is granted, it means that the court has dealt with parental consent to adoption: the consent has either been given or dispensed with by the court on one of the statutory grounds. As a result, consent to adoption should not be an issue in the subsequent adoption, and, to that extent, authority for adoption is similar to freeing. However, the overall effect of the permanence order with authority to adopt is not as rigid as freeing was. For instance, there may be an ancillary provision giving contact, direct or indirect, to the parents. And unlike a freeing order, a permanence order with authority to adopt makes a child looked after until the adoption is granted and the whole order ceases to have effect, or the order is otherwise revoked.

ss.80, 83, 102 and 100 2007 Act

6 Pre-court procedures

The decision to apply for a permanence order or permanence order with authority to adopt is taken by the local authority's "agency decision-maker" after their own internal reviews and administrative procedures. There are considerations or principles that apply to local authority planning for any permanence order or permanence order with authority to adopt application – see Chapter 2. Local authority duties are in s.17 of the 1995 Act and the LAC Regs 2009, because planning for a permanence order or permanence order with authority to adopt will almost always be work carried out for a looked after child, and any child subject to a permanence order or permanence order with authority to adopt is looked after.

s.17 1995 Act; LAC Regs 2009; and possibly Ad Ag Regs 2009

7 Adoption or fostering panels

7.1

When a permanence order is the plan for a child, the Ad Ag Regs 2009 do not apply to the local authority processes. This means that there is no duty on a local authority to take its plans for a permanence order to its adoption/permanence panel, although many local authorities choose to do this. Also, there are no timescales for any of the period between making the looked after review decision to seek permanence away from home and lodging the court application. When a permanence order is the plan, whether the case is considered by the panel or not, the authority makes a formal decision to apply to the court. This decision should be intimated to the parents and others as appropriate, including the child when they are older.

7.2

When a permanence order with authority to adopt is the plan for a child, the local authority must follow the processes set out in the Ad Ag Regs 2009 before applying to the court, because the overall plan is for adoption. Sometimes, a child may already be placed for adoption, but the local authority wishes to proceed with a permanence order with authority to adopt anyway, before the adoption application. However, a permanence order with authority to adopt is not mandatory for an agency adoption to go ahead.

Ad Ag Regs 2009

8 Procedural timescales

As in a direct agency adoption application, there are complicated regulations about procedures and timescales before a permanence order with authority to adopt may be applied for. The local authority must refer its plan for a permanence order with authority to adopt to its adoption/permanence panel, for a recommendation about whether adoption is in the child's best interests with a permanence order with authority to adopt, and registration of the child for adoption. There are then timescales from the panel recommendations being made through to notifications to parents and beyond, if the plan is opposed. If the birth parents indicate within a certain time that they are in agreement with the plan for adoption with a permanence order with authority to adopt, the agency can go ahead without further timescales. If, however, the parents refuse to agree, or do not return the notifications within a set time, the local authority is tied by strict timescales. It must apply for a permanence order with authority to adopt or ensure that an adoption application is lodged by adoptive parents within very short timescales.

Ad Ag Regs 2009, Regs 6, 12–17 and 20–23; also 18 and 23A

9 Child subject to a compulsory supervision order

When a child is subject to a compulsory supervision order and permanence plans are made, there are additional requirements. The plan may be for a permanence order on its own, or for adoption with or without a permanence order with authority to adopt. The child must be referred to a hearing for it to review the compulsory supervision order and provide written "advice" to the court about the plans. If adoption is planned, with or without a permanence order with authority to adopt, and the parents and/or the hearing do not agree with the plans, there are further detailed timescales.

ss.131, 137, 138 and 141 2011 Act; Ad Ag Regs 2009, Regs 22 and 23

10 Court report

In every permanence order and permanence order with authority to adopt application, the local authority must prepare and lodge a detailed report for the court with the application or petition. There are detailed court rules about what the report should cover.

Sheriff Court Adoption Rules 2009, r.31(2)(b) and (3); RCS r.67.28(2)(b) and (3)

11 Court procedures for permanence orders and permanence orders with authority to adopt

11.1

Permanence orders and permanence orders with authority to adopt may be applied for in the sheriff court or the Court of Session. In every application, whether agreed or not, the court has to be satisfied about a number of conditions and considerations, including the principles set out in Chapter 2. Court procedures for all permanence orders and permanence orders with authority to adopt are very similar to those for adoption applications. Where the child resides in Scotland, at the time an application is made for a permanence order or permanence order with authority to adopt, it may be heard in the Court of Session or in the local sheriff court. The decision about where to apply is made by the authority making the application. Most cases are dealt with in the sheriff court. If the child resides outwith Scotland at the time the application is made, the application must be made in the Court of Session and may only be for a permanence order with authority to adopt. It is not possible to apply for a permanence order when the child does not live in Scotland.

ss.83 and 84, 14 and 118 2007 Act

11.2

Forms are provided with the court rules for permanence order and permanence order with authority to adopt applications or petitions. These are in appendices to the rules, but the easiest way to obtain up-to-date versions is from the courts directly, or from the Scottish Courts website – see Further Reading. Forms are completed and lodged in court, along with other documents such as the child's birth certificate and the detailed local authority report.

Sheriff Court Adoption Rules 2009, r.31, especially r.31(2); RCS r.67.28, especially r.67.28(2)

11.3

Once the permanence order or permanence order with authority to adopt petition is lodged, court rules have timetables for dealing with the different stages of the application, particularly in disputed cases. The court arranges a preliminary hearing to take place within eight weeks, and will appoint a curator, and in permanence order with authority to adopt applications, also appoint a reporting officer. The applicant has to intimate the application and the hearing date to the child's parents and anyone else the court thinks should receive notice. Anyone who wishes to oppose the application must lodge a form of response saying this, within 21 days.

Sheriff Court Adoption Rules 2009, rr.32–38; RCS rr.67.29–67.32

12 Curator ad litem

The curator is an independent person providing a view of the case from the perspective of the child's welfare. They must also give the child's views to the court, provided the child wishes to give them to the curator. The curator is often the same person as the reporting officer, but not always. The curator should report back to the court within four weeks.

Sheriff Court Adoption Rules 2009, rr.32 and 44; RCS rr.67.29 and 67.38

13 Reporting officer

13.1

A reporting officer is appointed in all permanence order with authority to adopt cases but in permanence order applications only when the child is 12 or over. They are concerned with the consent or non-consent to the application. If a permanence order with authority to adopt is being sought, the reporting officer has to find out if the parents agree to adoption. When the application is for a permanence order or permanence order with authority to adopt and the child is aged 12 or over, the reporting officer also has to find out whether the child consents or not. When parents and/or the child agree with the application, the reporting officer obtains their formal written consents. If the parents and/or the child do not agree, the reporting officer reports this to the court. The reporting officer should report back to the court within four weeks.

Sheriff Court Adoption Rules 2009, r.32 and r.44; RCS r.67.29 and r.67.38

13.2

At the preliminary hearing, if there is no opposition to the application, the court may grant the order or continue the matter for further information, etc. Even when the child's parents have consented, the court must be satisfied about the principles in the 2007 Act – see Chapter 2 and paragraph 10 in this chapter. If there is no opposition in a permanence order with authority to adopt application, but the birth parents have not formally consented, the court will have to be satisfied that their consent may be dispensed with, although there may not be a full evidential proof – see paragraphs 11 and 12 in this chapter.

ss.84, 14 and 83 2007 Act; Sheriff Court Adoption Rules 2009, r.35; RCS, r.67.31

14 Legal threshold test for granting a permanence order

In every application for a permanence order or permanence order with authority to adopt, the court must take account of a range of principles, conditions and considerations. It must make its decision on the basis of the principles in the 2007 Act – see Chapter 2. When the child is 12 or over, the court must also be satisfied that they consent to the permanence order or permanence order with authority to adopt. As well as the principles, in every permanence order and permanence order with authority to adopt application, the court must also be satisfied that one of the "grounds" is established. These are *either* that there is no one who has the parental right to control the child's residence, that is the right to say where the child should live; *or*, if there is someone who has this right, that it would be 'seriously detrimental to the welfare of the child' for them to live with the person, that is, it would be 'seriously detrimental' for the child to live at home. The first ground will be satisfied if there is no parent with the right to control residence. However, in many cases, there will be at least one parent who has that right, so the local authority has to show that it would be 'seriously detrimental' for the child to return to live with the parent/s.

s.84, including s.84(5)(c), and s.14 for POA applications 2007 Act

15 Additional threshold test for granting a permanence order with authority to adopt

When the application is for a permanence order with authority to adopt, there are four additional tests that have to be met before a court may grant the order. These are in addition to those mentioned in paragraph 1.2 in this chapter, and Chapter 2. These additional matters are that:

- the local authority has asked for authority for adoption in their application;
- the court is satisfied that the child has been placed for adoption or is likely to be placed for adoption;
- the court is satisfied that either the parents consent to adoption, or the consent should be dispensed with; and
- the court thinks that it would be better for the child that it grants the authority for adoption rather than not grant it the "minimum necessary intervention" test.

s.83(1), with s.83(2)–(5) 2007 Act

16 Dispensing with parental consent

If the parents do not consent to the permanence order with authority to adopt and adoption, there are five grounds for dispensing with parental consent. They are the same as those used in adoption applications. The grounds are that:

- the parent or guardian is dead, s.83(2)(a);
- the parent or guardian cannot be found or is incapable of consenting, s.83(2)(b);
- the parent or guardian –
  - has parental responsibilities or rights and
  - cannot, in the court's opinion, 'satisfactorily...discharge' those parental responsibilities or exercise those parental rights and
  - 'is likely to continue to be unable to do so', s.83(3);
- the parent or guardian –
  - has lost all parental responsibilities or rights through a permanence order which does not give authority for adoption, (i.e. a permanence order not a permanence order with authority to adopt) and
  - is 'unlikely' to be given back such responsibilities or rights, s.83(4).
- Where neither of the previous two grounds (i.e. 3 and 4) apply, the child's welfare 'otherwise requires the consent to be dispensed with', s.83(2)(d).

s.83(1)(c), (2), (3), (4) and (5) 2007 Act

17 Opposition to application by parents

If the child's parents are opposing the application, the local authority must lodge a brief statement of the facts it will be relying on, and this must then be answered by or on behalf of the parents. A proof hearing will be fixed, which should be within 16 weeks, and a pre-proof hearing is also arranged in most cases, to enable the court to find out if the parties are properly prepared. In the sheriff court, Practice Notes for each Sheriffdom give further directions about procedures to be followed – see Further Reading.

Sheriff Court Adoption Rules 2009, rr.34A–37; RCS rr.67.31 and 67.32

18 Disputed permanence order

In a disputed permanence order, when the child's parents are opposing the application, the court considers all the evidence about the case. If the court is satisfied evidentially, it still has to decide whether to grant the permanence order, on the basis of the welfare and other principles (see Chapter 2).

19 Disputed permanence order with authority to adopt

In a disputed permanence order with authority to adopt, when the child's parents are opposing the application, the local authority has to ask the court to dispense with its consent on one of the grounds listed in s.83(2)–(4) of the 2007 Act. The court considers all the evidence in order to decide whether to dispense with consent on one of the grounds listed in paragraph 16 in this chapter. If the court is satisfied evidentially, it still has to decide whether to dispense with the consent, and then whether to grant the permanence order with authority to adopt, on the basis of the welfare and other principles (see Chapter 2).

20 Revocation of compulsory supervision order

When a court grants a permanence order or a permanence order with authority to adopt and the child is subject to a compulsory supervision order, the court must revoke the compulsory supervision order unless it thinks the child still needs compulsory measures under the children's hearing system.

s.89 2007 Act

21 Right of appeal

When a court grants a permanence order or a permanence order with authority to adopt or refuses to grant an order, there is a right of appeal. If the application was made in the sheriff court, an appeal may be made to the Sheriff Principal and/or to the Inner House of the Court of Session. If the application was made in the Court of Session, an appeal may be made to the Inner House of the Court of Session. A further appeal is possible to the Supreme Court.

22 Children's hearings and permanence orders

If there is a pending court application for a permanence order, permanence order with authority to adopt, amendment or variation, there are restrictions on the decisions that children's hearings may make about the child. If a hearing wants to vary an existing compulsory supervision order for the child or make a new compulsory supervision order, it cannot do so unless the court agrees. The hearing makes its decision and must then prepare a report for the court about its intentions. There are regulations about the contents of the report and rules about the court process. The provisions are complex and cause difficulties, especially when the child has been matched for an adoption placement.

ss.95 and 96 2007 Act; Adoption and Children (Scotland) Act 2007 (Supervision Requirement Reports in Applications for Permanence Orders) Regulations 2009, SSI 2009/169; Sheriff Court Adoption Rules 2009, r.51; RCS rr.67.43

23 Compulsory supervision order during court process

When there is a permanence order or permanence order with authority to adopt for a child, and the child is also the subject of a compulsory supervision order, the local authority must not act incompatibly with the compulsory supervision order.

s.90 2007 Act

24 Effects of permanence orders and permanence orders with authority to adopt

The effect of each permanence order or permanence order with authority to adopt depends on the order's particular terms, but every child subject to either of these orders is looked after by the local authority. Every order gives the local authority the mandatory provision – see paragraph 3 in this chapter – so the local authority controls where the child lives.

The effect of a permanence order with ancillary provision otherwise depends on what is in the order, how many other rights and responsibilities have been given to the local authority and/or others such as carers, and how many have been taken away from the parents. The effect of a permanence order with authority to adopt also partly depends on what the ancillary provisions are. But every permanence order with authority to adopt has authority for adoption, so the child's parents' consent to adoption has been dealt with and should not be an issue in the subsequent adoption.

s.17(6) as amended 1995 Act; ss.80–82 and ss.87 and 88 2007 Act

25 Section 11 applications

When there is a permanence order or a permanence order with authority to adopt for a child, there are restrictions on the use of s.11 of the 1995 Act. A court may not make an order under s.11, unless the application is for an interdict, appointment of a judicial factor for the child or appointment or removal of someone as the child's guardian. This is because the permanence order or permanence order with authority to adopt sets out who has what PRRs, and any changes should be applied for in a variation or revocation of that order.

s.11A 1995 Act inserted by s.103 2007 Act

26 Variation, amendment and revocation of permanence orders and permanence orders with authority to adopt

A permanence order or permanence order with authority to adopt may have its ancillary provisions varied, or it may be revoked. A permanence order may be amended to have authority for adoption added. When there is any application for variation, amendment or revocation of a permanence order or permanence order with authority to adopt, the court must apply three of the general principles referred to in Chapter 2. It must:

- treat the child's welfare through childhood (or life if an amendment is sought) as its paramount consideration;
- seek and take account of the child's views, bearing in mind their age and maturity; and

- have regard to the child's religious persuasion, racial, cultural and linguistic heritage.

ss.92, 93 and 98 2007 Act, referring back to s.84(4), (5)(a) and (b) and (6)

27 Variation, amendment or revocation of order

27.1 Variation of order

Local authorities that hold a permanence order or permanence order with authority to adopt must apply to court for variation of the ancillary provisions or for revocation of the order in certain circumstances. These are if there has been a "material change" in relation to matters covered in the order, provided they think that the change means the order should be varied or revoked.

s.99 2007 Act

27.2

Anyone with an interest, including the child, the child's parents and the local authority, may apply to the sheriff for variation of the ancillary provisions of a permanence order or permanence order with authority to adopt. However, everyone, except the local authority, must have leave of the court to go ahead with a full application. Leave must be granted if the court is satisfied 'that there has been a material change of circumstance' or if there is another reason to allow the application to go ahead. When deciding whether to grant leave, the court has to take account of the child's welfare and the circumstances of the child's parents, anyone with some PRRs and others. If there are no ancillary provisions in the original order, no variation is possible.

ss.92, 94(4)–(6) 2007 Act

27.3 Amendment of order

Local authorities that hold a permanence order may apply to amend the order by having authority for adoption added. In other words, they may ask the court to make it a permanence order with authority to adopt. The court must be satisfied about three of the four matters listed in paragraph 15 in this chapter. These are that the child has been placed for adoption or is likely to be placed for adoption; the parents consent to an adoption, or the consent should be dispensed with; and it would be better for the child that there is authority for adoption rather than not. If parental consent to adoption is not given, the court may dispense with it on the basis of the same grounds as in a permanence order with authority to adopt or adoption application – see paragraph 16 in this chapter. If the amendment is granted, the permanence order becomes a permanence order with authority to adopt.

s.93(2)–(4) referring back to s.83 2007 Act

27.4 Revocation of order

The local authority or any other person affected by the order may apply to the sheriff for revocation of a permanence order or permanence order with authority to adopt. However, everyone, except the local authority, must have leave of the court to go ahead with a full application. The court may revoke the order if it is satisfied that it is appropriate in all the circumstances, including any material changes and the wishes of parents about having PRRs given to people who have them under the order. If the court revokes the order, it must consider whether to make orders under s.11 of the 1995 Act, about PRRs.

s.98 referring back to ss.84 and 100 2007 Act

27.5

If a permanence order or permanence order with authority to adopt is not revoked, it lasts until the child is 18, unless they are adopted before then. The right to determine the child's place of residence ceases when the child is 16.

ss.102 and 81 2007 Act

13

Adoption

This chapter deals briefly with some aspects of adoption in Scotland. Intercountry adoption and other foreign adoption matters are covered in another chapter.

1 General information

Adoption in Scotland was introduced under the Adoption (Scotland) Act 1930. There have been a number of subsequent provisions, including the Adoption (Scotland) Act 1978, which was substantially amended in 1997 by the 1995 Act. On 28 September 2009, the Adoption and Children (Scotland) Act 2007 replaced the 1978 Act. The 2007 Act followed the Adoption Policy Review Group Review, particularly the 2005 Phase II Report. The Adoption and Children Act 2002, the main legislation for England and Wales from 30 December 2005, only applies in Scotland in a few matters.

APRG 2005 Phase II Report; 2007 Act; Adoption and Children Act 2002

2 Effect of adoption

Adoption of a child is a legal process where a child's birth family is replaced in law by a new adoptive family, cutting off all legal ties and links with the birth family. The child becomes as if born into the adoptive family.

s.40 2007 Act

3 Who may be adopted?

For a child to be adopted, they must be under 18 and unmarried. However, if an adoption petition has been lodged before a child's 18th birthday, it may be dealt with and granted even after the child reaches that age. The child may be of any nationality. The consent of a child aged 12 or over is formally required before the order may be granted. This may only be dispensed with if the court considers the child is incapable of consenting.

ss.28(4) and 32 2007 Act

4 Who may adopt?

4.1

There is no upper age limit for adoption, although many adoption agencies impose one, but there are lower age limits. People under 21 cannot adopt, but if the adopter is a step-parent, adoption is allowed provided the birth parent is 18, although the step-parent must be over 21. Adopters must *either* be domiciled in the UK (i.e. consider it as their long-term permanent home, even if they do not currently live there) *or* have been habitually resident in the UK for more than one year prior to the application. Where a couple are adopting, only one of them needs to be domiciled in the UK if that is the eligibility test they are using. Adopters do not have to have British nationality to be eligible to adopt.

ss.29 and 30 2007 Act

4.2

Adopters are either a couple or a single person. A couple can adopt together if they are married or are civil partners or are living together "in an enduring family relationship" as if married or civil partners. In step-parent adoptions, the step-parent applies on their own, and it is no longer possible for them to adopt *with* the birth parent.

ss.29 and 30 2007 Act

5 Consent by parents

In order for a child to be adopted, every parent with PRRs must either consent to the adoption or have their consent dispensed with. The consent is dealt with in the adoption application, or it may be done in an earlier court process for a permanence order with authority to adopt.

ss.31, 80, 83 and 84, and 32 and 84(1) 2007 Act

6 Legislation and regulations

Adoption and permanence order with authority to adopt applications are dealt with in the 2007 Act. There is a range of adoption regulations, including for adoption agencies, adoption support services and allowances, accessing adoption-related information and foreign adoptions. The Health and Social Care Standards[42] include standards for adoption.[43] There are also rules of court for the sheriff court and the Court of Session. And there are Practice Notes for each sheriffdom, designed 'to secure the efficient management of contested applications and other proceedings under the 2007 Act' – see Further Reading.

2007 Act; Ad Ag Regs 2009; Ad Supp Regs 2009; Ad Info Regs 2009; Foreign Adoption Regs 2009; Adoption Standards; Sheriff Court Adoption Rules 2009; RCS 1994, Ch 67

7 Principles to be applied

The general principles apply to all decisions made by courts and adoption agencies about adoption and permanence orders with authority to adopt. These include all the circumstances of the case and planning decisions by agencies. The child's welfare throughout their life is the paramount consideration. The child's views must be sought and given regard to by agencies and courts and there must be consideration of religion, race, culture and language. Agencies and courts must also consider other options for the child and decide on

42 Health and Social Care Standards: My support, my life (2017), https://www.gov.scot/publications/health-social-care-standards-support-life/

43 A Quality Framework for Fostering, Adoption and Adult Placement Services (2021), https://www.careinspectorate.com/images/documents/6098/Quality%20framework%20for%20fostering%20and%20adoption%20and%20adult%20placement%20services%202021.pdf

adoption only if it is the best choice. This does not mean that adoption is a last resort. Attention must be given to the value of a stable family unit in the child's development and the likely effect on the child, throughout the child's life of the making of an adoption order.

ss.14, 28(2) and 84 2007 Act

8 Routes to adoption

8.1 Direct petition

An adoption order may be granted where adopters apply directly to the court to adopt a specific child. They will usually instruct solicitors to present the petition on their behalf.

ss.28–30 2007 Act

8.2 Permanence order with authority to adopt (POA)

The local authority applies to the court for a permanence order with authority to adopt. Thereafter, once this is granted, the adoptive parents need to petition the court to adopt the child.

A permanence order with authority to adopt deals with parental consent to adoption prior to the actual adoption application. If a local authority is planning adoption for a child, it may choose to deal with parental consent in a permanence order with authority to adopt application process, before placing with adopters, or to avoid a direct dispute between birth parents and adopters over a child already placed. However, obtaining such an order is not mandatory and it is not necessary for there to be one of these for a child before they are placed or adopted.

ss.80–84 and 31 2007 Act

9 Adoption agencies

There are two types of adoption agencies:

- **local authority adoption agencies**;
- **registered adoption services**. These are voluntary agencies providing adoption services and must operate on a not-for-profit basis. They were formerly approved by the Scottish Executive under the 1978 Act, then registered and inspected by the Care Commission from April 2004.

Both types of agencies are now registered with and inspected by the Care Inspectorate under the 2010 Act. All agencies must have an adoption panel unless they do not plan for children or assess adopters.

ss.1 and 2 2007 Act; ss.83 and 59 2010 Act, incl s.59(3); Regs 3–6 Ad Ag Regs 2009

10 Inspections

All local authorities have a duty to have their own adoption agency and to provide an adoption service for their area, including provision for intercountry adoption (and adoption support). They have to provide adoption services along with their other social work provision and with registered adoption services operating in their area. Local authority adoption agencies and registered adoption services must be registered with and inspected by the Care Inspectorate.

Local authorities set out their adoption services in their Adoption Services Plans, which may or may not be part of their wider Children's Services Plans. The 2014 Act replaced these duties.

ss.1, 2, 9–12 and 4 2007 Act; ss.83 and 59 2010 Act; ss.7–18 2014 Act

11 Types of adoption

11.1

The 2007 Act provides for two types of adoption:

- agency adoptions; and
- relative and step-parent adoptions.

An agency adoption is where an adoption agency places a child for adoption. The child will usually, but not always, be looked after. A relative adoption can be applied for by a grandparent, brother, sister, uncle, aunt of the full or half blood, and by affinity, which means by marriage or civil partnership. This includes the father of the child and his relatives if the father was not married to the mother. In a step-parent adoption, the adopter must be married to or in a civil partnership with or living in an "enduring family relationship" with the birth parent who has PRRs. Most non-agency adoptions are step-parent ones.

s.75, s.119(1) and ss.29 and 30 2007 Act

11.2

Strictly speaking, no adoption should be arranged by anyone other than an adoption agency, unless it is a relative or step-parent one. However, in some circumstances, an adoption order may be granted when the child was not placed by an agency and is not being adopted by a close relative. For example, foster carers may seek to adopt a child who was placed with them under the fostering regulations, but not the adoption regulations. And intercountry adoptions are not agency ones, even though the adopters will have been assessed and approved by an agency.

ss.75 and 72 2007 Act

11.3

In practice, most adoptions are either arranged by local authorities or other agencies, or are "relative" ones, mainly involving step-parents. The legal requirements and processes for both types of adoption are much the same, although some specific issues are different between the two types.

12 Pre-court procedures: non-agency adoptions

In *all* non-agency adoptions, including relative and step-parent ones, and intercountry adoptions, applicants must notify the local authority where they live about their intention to adopt. The notification must be made at least three months before the adoption order is granted.

s.18 2007 Act

12.1 Lodging reports

The local authority must prepare and lodge in court a report about the family, the child and all the circumstances of the case. This is often referred to as "s.19 Report". There are detailed court rules about what the report should cover.

s.19 2007 Act; Sheriff Court Adoption Rules 2009, r.8(4)–(7); RCS r.67.8(4)–(7)

12.2 Adoptions with a foreign element

In some step-parent or relative adoptions, the child has come from overseas and there may be some international aspects to the adoption, such as the need to obtain written consent from a birth parent who resides abroad. These adoptions are not intercountry ones and the adopters do not have to have been assessed under the intercountry adoption rules. Similarly, when a child is brought into the UK from overseas by people who have been living and working abroad, and who then wish to adopt the child, that is not an intercountry adoption. Court rules have provisions about having agreements signed abroad when this is necessary.

Sheriff Court Adoption Rules 2009, r.13(3)(c); RCS r.67.13(3)(c)

13 Pre-court procedures: agency adoptions

13.1

Where a local authority wishes to place a child for adoption, with or without a permanence order with authority to adopt application, there are complicated regulations about procedures and timescales. The adoption agency's crucial stages are the adoption panel and the agency decision-maker.

13.2

No child may be placed unless an agency's adoption panel has considered the plans for the child and made a recommendation that adoption, with or without a permanence order with authority to adopt, is the best plan for the child.

13.3

In every case, disputed or undisputed, the agency then has timescales within which it must make a formal decision and notify this to birth parents and others. If the birth parents indicate within a certain time that they are in agreement with the plan for adoption and/or a permanence order with authority to adopt, the agency may go ahead without further timescales. If, however, the parents refuse to agree, or do not return the notifications within a set time, the agency is tied by strict timescales. It must apply for a permanence order with authority to adopt within very short timescales. There are also general duties on agencies about placing a child, about information gathering, notifications and visiting.

Ad Ag Regs 2009, Reg 6, Regs 12–17 and 20–23; also Regs 18 and 23A–25A

13.4 Advice from children's hearings for a child subject to a compulsory supervision order

When a child is subject to a compulsory supervision order and adoption plans, with or without a permanence order with authority to adopt, there are additional requirements. The child must be referred to a children's hearing for a review of the compulsory supervision order and consideration of the plans. The hearing provides a written report on the plans, usually called "advice". Where the parent does not agree, and/or the hearing members disagree with the plans, there are detailed timescales which apply.

ss.131, 137, 138 and 141 2011 Act; and Ad Ag Regs 2009, Regs 22 and 23

13.5 Lodging reports

In all agency adoptions, the placing agency (and this includes English, Welsh and Northern Irish agencies when a child is placed from outwith Scotland) must prepare and lodge a report for the court. This is often referred to as a "s.17 Report", but it is almost the same as a "s.19 Report". There are the same detailed court rules about what the report should cover.

s.17 2007 Act; Sheriff Court Adoption Rules 2009, r.8(4)–(7); RCS r.67.8(4)–(7)

14 Court procedures

Adoption may be applied for in the sheriff court or the Court of Session. In every application, whether agreed or not, the court has to be satisfied about a number of conditions and considerations. Court procedures for adoption, and all permanence orders with authority to adopt and permanence orders, are very similar. Where the child resides in Scotland at the time an adoption application is made, it may be heard in the Court of Session or in any sheriff court within the local jurisdiction. The decision about where to apply is made by the adopter making the application. Most cases are dealt with in the sheriff court. If the child resides outwith Scotland at the time the application is made, it can only be heard in the Court of Session.

s.118 2007 Act

15 Court forms

Forms are provided with the court rules for adoption, permanence order and permanence order with authority to adopt applications or petitions. These are in appendices to the rules, but the easiest way to obtain up-to-date versions is from the courts directly, or from the Scottish Courts website – see Further Reading. Forms are completed and lodged in court, along with other documents such as the child's birth certificate. The s.17 or s.19 report should also be lodged at the same time. In permanence order and permanence order with authority to adopt cases, the local authority also has to lodge a detailed report with every court application.

Sheriff Court Adoption Rules 2009, r.8, especially r.8(3)(d) and (e); RCS r.67.8, especially r.67.8(3)(d) and (e)

16 Time requirements

Once the adoption petition is lodged, court rules have timetables for dealing with the different stages of the application, particularly in disputed cases. The court arranges a preliminary hearing to take place within six to eight weeks. The applicant must then intimate the application and the hearing date to the birth parents and anyone else the court thinks should receive notice. Anyone who wishes to oppose the application must lodge a form of response saying this, within 21 days. The court also appoints a curator, and in most cases, a reporting officer.

Sheriff Court Adoption Rules 2009, rr.11, rr.14–16A, r.18, r.18A, r.19, r.20 and r.22; RCS r.67.11, rr.67.14 and 67.15 and rr.67.17 and 67.18

17 Preliminary hearing

At the preliminary hearing, if there is no opposition to the application, the court may grant the order or continue the matter for further information, etc. Even when the birth parents have consented, the court must be satisfied about the principles in the 2007 Act. If there is no opposition but the birth parents have not formally consented, the court will have to be satisfied that the consent may be dispensed with, although there may not be a full evidential proof.

ss.14, 28(2) and 31 2007 Act; Sheriff Court Adoption Rules 2009, r.18; RCS, r.67.17

18 Fixing of proof hearing

If the birth parents are opposing the application, the adopters must lodge a brief statement of the facts they will be relying on, and this must then be answered by or on behalf of the birth parents. A proof hearing will be fixed, which should be within 16 weeks. A pre-proof hearing is also arranged in most cases, to enable the court to find out if the parties are properly prepared. In the sheriff court, Practice Notes for each Sheriffdom give further directions about procedures to be followed – see Further Reading.

Sheriff Court Adoption Rules 2009, r.16A and rr.18–20; RCS, rr.67.17 and 67.18

19 Reporting officer

The reporting officer is mainly concerned with the consent or non-consent to the adoption by the parents and by any child aged 12 or over. When parents and/or the child agree to the adoption, the reporting officer obtains their formal written consents. When there is no agreement, they report this to the court. The reporting officer should report back to the court within four weeks. No reporting officer is appointed if there is a permanence order with authority to adopt and the child is under 12.

Sheriff Court Adoption Rules 2009, rr.11 and 12; RCS rr.67.11 and 67.12

20 Curator ad litem

20.1

The court also appoints a curator who should report back to the court within four weeks. The curator is often the same person as the reporting officer, but not always. The curator is an independent person providing a view of the case from the perspective of the child's welfare. They must also give the child's views to the court, provided the child wishes to give them to the curator.

Sheriff Court Adoption Rules 2009, rr.11 and 12; RCS rr.67.11 and 67.12

20.2

Before any child may be adopted, every parent with PRRs must:

- formally consent to the adoption; or
- have their consent dispensed with in the adoption application on the basis of one or more of the five grounds in s.31(3)–(6); or
- have had their consent fully dealt with in an earlier court case, such as a permanence order with authority to adopt, or a freeing order (in Northern Ireland); or

- have had their consent partially dealt with in earlier proceedings under the Adoption and Children Act 2002 (in England or Wales), and they do not dispute the adoption application.

s.31 2007 Act

20.3

There are five grounds for dispensing with consent, and they are the same as those used in permanence order with authority to adopt applications. They are different from those in the previous legislation and are also different from those used in England and Wales under the 2002 Act. The grounds are:

1. *the parent or guardian is dead, s.31(3)(a);*
2. *the parent or guardian cannot be found or is incapable of consenting, s.31(3)(b);*
3. *the parent or guardian*
   - *has parental responsibilities or rights or*
   - *cannot, in the court's opinion, 'satisfactorily...discharge' those parental responsibilities or exercise those parental rights and*
   - *'is likely to continue to be unable to do so', s.31(4);*
4. *the parent or guardian*
   - *has lost all parental responsibilities or rights through a permanence order which does not give authority for adoption (i.e. a PO not a POA) and*
   - *is 'unlikely' to be given back such responsibilities or rights, s.31(5);*
5. *where neither of the previous two grounds (i.e. 3 and 4) apply, the child's welfare 'otherwise requires the consent to be dispensed with', s.31(3)(d).*

s.31(3)–(6) 2007 Act

21 Dispensing with parental consent

If the parents are disputing the adoption, the adopters have to ask the court to dispense with their consent on one of the grounds listed in s.31 of the 2007 Act, if consent has not already been dealt with in an earlier court case. The court considers evidence in order to decide whether to dispense with consent on one of the grounds listed in paragraph 20.3 in this chapter. If the court is satisfied evidentially, it still has to decide on the basis of the welfare and other principles whether to dispense with the consent, and then whether to grant the adoption. The court's decision about the application (apart from whether there is sufficient evidence to dispense with consent) is governed by the principles in the 2007 Act.

22 Consideration of revocation of compulsory supervision order

Where a court grants an adoption order and the child is subject to a compulsory supervision order, the court must revoke the order unless it thinks that the child still needs compulsory measures under the children's hearing system.

s.36 2007 Act

23 Rights of appeal

When a court grants or refuses to grant an adoption order, there is a right of appeal. If the application was made in the sheriff court, an appeal may be made to the Sheriff Appeal Court (civil) or, with leave, to the Court of Session. While further appeal to the Supreme Court is rare, there have been a couple of notable appeals which have served to clarify this complicated area of the law.

24 Effects of an adoption order

When an adoption order is granted in favour of a couple or an individual, that person or those persons hold all the PRRs over the child as if the child had been born to them. The birth parents, if they have not previously lost all PRRs through a permanence order with authority to adopt process, now lose all formal responsibilities for and rights to their child. There may be ongoing contact arrangements by agreement with the adopters. It is possible to have a contact condition attached to an adoption order, but this is not common and will normally only happen in "exceptional" circumstances. After an adoption, birth parents cannot use s.11 of the 1995 Act except to apply for a contact order, and they must have leave of the court before they may even go ahead and apply fully.

ss.40 and 28(3) 2007 Act; s.11(3)–(6) 1995 Act as amended by the 2007 Act

25 Support services

Local authority adoption agencies have a duty to provide adoption support to a wide range of people affected by adoption, including adopted children and adults, adopters and their children, and the birth families of adopted children and adults. The adoption support system was widened under the 2007 Act with the intention of extending the system and ensuring greater uniformity of services. The Ad Supp Regulations 2009 and the 2007 Act Guidance are also relevant. The system is complex and covers agency and non-agency adoptions.

s.1, ss.9–12 and 45–52 2007 Act; Ad Supp Regs 2009; 2007 Act Guidance

26 Local authority's duty to support child and parents

Children being adopted, their adopters and their birth parents may receive support services without assessments of their need for these. There are adoption support plans, which are possible for any family with adopted children under 18. Adoption allowances are available for agency adopters in certain circumstances.

s.1, ss.9–12 and ss.45–52 2007 Act; Ad Supp Regs 2009, particularly Reg 4

27 Support for those affected by adoption

A wide range of other people are also eligible for assessments of their needs for adoption support, including counselling and service provision if there is need.

Overall, these duties are wide and apply to the whole of the local authorities where people seeking services live. In addition, they apply to all adoptions, agency and non-agency, past and present. For example, when a birth parent wants help about tracing a child who has been adopted, they are entitled to an assessment of need for support by the local authority in whose area they currently live.

Other members of birth families and people affected by adoption are also entitled to assessments for adoption support services. These duties clearly cover providing help to birth families about ways of tracing family members who have been adopted.

s.1, ss.9–12 2007 Act; Ad Supp Regs 2009, particularly Regs 5–9

28 Accessing adoption records – child

In Scotland, when an adopted person reaches 16, they have automatic rights of access to:

- their original birth certificate;
- their court process from the adoption, and from any permanence order with authority to adopt as well; and
- their adoption agency records, if the adoption was an agency one.

Counselling services are available but optional. An adopted person will be entitled to adoption support services to help them find this information and decide what other steps, if any, to take. They should formally request support services to help access any adoption agency records, but the other information may be sought without this, although support may be helpful.

s.55 2007 Act; Sheriff Court Adoption Rules 2009, r.25(2)(a) and r.39(2) and (3)(a); RCS, r.67.21(2)(a) and r.67.33(2) and (3)(a); Ad Info Regs 2009, Regs 3(1) and 4

29 Accessing adoption records – others

Adoption agencies also have a general discretion to provide access to their records as part of their functions as agencies, including to other local authorities that have been approached by adopted people for help in accessing their records. There is no right of access to information for birth parents.

Ad Info Regs 2009, Reg 3(2)–(5), and Regs 4–6

30 Exemptions – data protection

Adoption agency records are exempt from the subject access provisions of the GDPR 2018, so there is no right of subject access to them. Instead, adoption records are accessed under the Adoption Information Regulations 2009.

Data Protection Act 2018 Schedule 4(3)

14

Foreign adoptions

This chapter gives some basic information about foreign adoptions, including intercountry adoptions. It deals with two situations:

- where a child from overseas is adopted into Scotland, usually referred to as intercountry adoption; and
- where a Scottish child leaves the UK for adoption in an overseas country.

Some adoptions have international aspects, e.g. step-parent adoption of a child from overseas now living in the UK with their parent and step-parent; step-parent adoption by someone domiciled in the UK but living abroad; and adoption by people who have returned to live in the UK after working abroad, where they adopted a child but that adoption is not recognised here. Although there may be difficulties in such cases, like obtaining parental consent from abroad or other logistical problems, these are not overseas or intercountry adoptions, but are ordinary "domestic" adoptions.

1 Intercountry adoption

1.1

Intercountry adoption is where a child from overseas is adopted into Scotland. Although the practice and policy about intercountry adoption are the same throughout the UK, there are a number of detailed differences between the system in Scotland and that for England and Wales. As a result, not all legal details provided on a UK basis are correct for Scotland.

1.2

Intercountry adoption is the term used by professionals, adoption agencies, central government and those who adopt children from outwith the UK. It refers to adoption where:

- the adopter/s reside in the UK; and
- the child resides in a country outside the UK (the State of origin); and
- the adopter/s either:
  - bring the child into the UK for the purposes of adoption or
  - adopt the child in their State of origin, *and* that order is recognised as adoption in UK law.

1.3

Other adoptions have international aspects, e.g. adoption of a step-child from overseas now living in the UK; or by adopters who have returned to live in the UK after working abroad, where they adopted a child but that adoption is not recognised here. However, these are not intercountry adoptions – see the introductory paragraphs to this chapter.

2 Background

2.1

Intercountry adoption in the UK was the subject of good practice procedures for some years but the system had no statutory basis. During the 1990s, there were increasing concerns about abuses and the UK had to legislate to enable it to ratify the Hague Convention.

2.2

The 1999 Act was passed to provide a regulatory system for intercountry adoption from the three groups of countries listed below. There are differences in the rules for each of the three groups of cases, although the underlying assessment processes are the same. In Scotland, the 1999 Act amended and added to the 1978 Act for intercountry purposes and provided for regulations and court rules to be made for these adoptions. The regulations, court rules and commencement orders for Scotland were different from those for England and Wales. Most, but not all, of the 1999 Act has been replaced in Scotland by the provisions of the 2007 Act.

1999 Act, as amended by and partially repealed by the 2007 Act

3 Types of countries from which children are adopted

3.1

There are three different types of countries from which intercountry adoptions are arranged, that is, three types of States of origin for children. The type of country of origin affects whether there has to be an adoption application in the UK after the child comes here. The three types of countries of origin are:

- **Convention countries:** countries that have implemented the Hague Convention. In some cases, the child will be adopted in the State of origin, in others adoption will be in the UK;
- **designated list countries:** countries on the designated list, whose adoption orders are recognised in the UK. There is no need for an adoption application here;
- **non-Convention/non-designated countries:** countries that are neither Hague Convention nor designated list ones. When the child enters the UK, it is necessary to apply to adopt here.

3.2

The Scottish Government and Department for Education (DfE) intercountry adoption websites (see Further Reading) list Convention and designated countries under 'Frequently asked questions'. The list of designated countries has been restated with effect from 3 January 2014. The Adoption (Designation of Overseas Adoptions) Order 1973 as varied by the Adoption (Designation of Overseas Adoptions) (Variation) (Scotland) Order 1995 has been revoked although that does not affect any adoption designated under it as an overseas one prior to 3 January 2014. There is an equivalent order for England and Wales.

Adoption (Recognition of Overseas Adoptions) (Scotland) Regulations 2013, SSI 2013/310, as amended by the Adoption (Recognition of Overseas Adoptions) (Scotland) Amendment Regulations 2013, SSI 2013/335

4 Special restrictions on countries

The Scottish Government has the power to make regulations imposing restrictions on adoptions from overseas countries as it sees necessary. These restrictions are to make sure that, when there are concerns about adoption practices in other countries, arrangements to adopt from these may be prohibited or restricted. There are special restrictions in relation to adoptions from Haiti, Nepal, Cambodia and Guatemala.

ss.62–65 2007 Act; Adoptions with a Foreign Element (Special Restrictions on Adoptions from Abroad) (Scotland) Regulations 2008, SSI 2008/303

5 Intercountry adoption processes: pre-court

5.1

In adoption from all three types of countries, prospective adopters, including close relatives, must have a home study prepared and be assessed as intercountry adopters by an adoption agency, either a local authority or a voluntary agency. Local authorities must provide an intercountry service. The assessment cannot be done by an independent social worker who is not commissioned by an adoption agency. The home study is for adoption from a specific country. After assessment, the agency takes the prospective adopters to its adoption panel and then the agency decision-maker approves them as intercountry adopters for the specific country, or does not approve them. When there is approval, the papers are sent by the agency to the Scottish Government.

s.1 2007 Act; Foreign Adoption Regs 2009; Ad Ag Regs 2009

5.2

If the proposed adoption is from a Convention country, the Scottish Government is the Central Authority. It processes the papers and if it agrees that an application can go ahead, the papers are passed to the Home Office for immigration clearance. Once this is completed, the Scottish Government as Central Authority passes the papers to the Central Authority for the State of origin and the prospective adopters can make arrangements there.

5.3

If the proposed adoption is from a designated or non-Convention/non-designated country, the process is the same, except the Central Authority is the DfE in London. So the papers go from the Scottish Government to the DfE and then on to the Home Office.

5.4

After completion of the arrangements in the State of origin, the adopters bring the child into the UK. If the adopters have not gone through the above processes, they may be guilty of an offence under the 2007 Act or the Foreign Adoption Regs 2009. There are four possible situations on return to the UK. The child will have been:

1. adopted in a Convention country (a Convention adoption);
2. brought in from a Convention country for adoption here by way of a Convention adoption order application;
3. adopted in a designated list country,
4. brought in from a non-Convention/non-designated country for adoption

here under the 2007 Act, s.29 or 30.

ss.58 and 61 2007 Act; Foreign Adoption Regs 2009, Reg 53; s.119(1) 2007 Act; 1999 Act

6 Intercountry adoption processes: court

6.1

In the first or third situations, there is no court application here, as both types of adoption are recognised in UK law. In the second or fourth situations, there has to be an adoption application here. It is also necessary in these two situations for the adopters to contact their local authority to advise that the child is living with them and give notice of:

- a private fostering arrangement under the 1984 Act; and
- their intention to adopt, under s.18 of the 2007 Act.

1984 Act; s.18 2007 Act

6.2

If the child has been brought in for adoption from a Convention country, a Convention adoption order application is made under the Foreign Adoption Regs 2009. This can be in the sheriff court or the Court of Session, and there are specific court rules for these applications.

Foreign Adoption Regs 2009, Reg 53; Sheriff Court Adoption Rules 2009, rr.28–30; RCS, rr.67.24–67.27

6.3

If the child has been brought in for adoption from a non-Convention/non-designated country, the case is similar to a domestic application, under the 1978 Act and the normal court rules.

s.29 or 30 2007 Act; Sheriff Court Adoption Rules 2009, rr.8–27; RCS rr.67.8–67.23

7 Residence period required before adoption can be granted in Scotland

There are rules about how long a child must live with both adopters before an order can be granted (not applied for). These are in s.15 of the 2007 Act. The period for intercountry adoptions is six months' residence.

s.15, particularly s.15(5) 2007 Act

8 Entry clearance and acquiring British citizenship

8.1

The Immigration Rules are extremely complex and specialist immigration advice should be sought. The UK Border Agency has a leaflet about intercountry adoption on its website, dated 2008. All intercountry adopters, including from Convention countries, should ensure that they have entry clearance for the child, in advance of bringing them into the UK.

8.2

In stranger intercountry adoptions, the basic rules about citizenship are relatively straightforward, and depend on the type of State of origin and where the adoption took place, i.e. in the UK or abroad.

- Convention adoption abroad confers British citizenship other than by descent (BC-OTB), provided one adopter is a British citizen and both are "habitually resident" in the UK.
- Convention adoption *and* non-Convention/non-designated adoption in the UK confers BC-OTB, provided one adopter is a British citizen.
- Designated adoption abroad does not automatically confer BC-OTBD. However, the adopters may apply to register the child as a British citizen

under the British Nationality Act 1981, and if successful, BC-OTBD will be conferred.

9 Registration of foreign adoptions

The Registration of Foreign Adoptions (Scotland) Regulations 2003 came into force on 1 June 2003. They allow adopters who have adopted abroad from Convention and designated countries to apply for an entry in the Scottish Adopted Children Register. The Registrar General will issue an extract from the Register. When a child has been adopted abroad, and the adoption is recognised in the UK, an entry in the Register may be made and an "ordinary" Scottish Extract Birth Certificate will be issued. The 2003 Regulations may be used for foreign adoptions which took place before June 2003.

Registration of Foreign Adoptions (Scotland) Regulations 2003, SSI 2003/67

10 Arrangements for Scottish children to be adopted overseas

10.1

These are covered by ss.59 and 60 of the 2007 Act, and the Foreign Adoptions Regs 2009 are also relevant. The provisions are complex and their effect is different from that under the 1978 Act, which allowed close relatives to take a child out of the UK for adoption abroad.

ss.59 and 60 2007 Act; Foreign Adoptions Regs 2009

10.2

It is an offence to take a "protected child" out of Great Britain for adoption overseas or to make arrangements for such an adoption. However, such an adoption is permitted if the child is taken out of Great Britain under a s.59 order or the equivalent provisions in other UK legislation. A "protected child" is a child who is habitually resident in the UK or is a Commonwealth citizen.

s.60 2007 Act

10.3

An s.59 order allows a child to be adopted abroad after a court application in Scotland. It gives the prospective adopters parental responsibilities and rights. An application may be made in the sheriff court or the Court of Session and the court rules treat them almost the same as domestic adoptions. However, a s.59 order cannot be made unless requirements in that section and the Foreign Adoptions Regs 2009 have been met. These include that the child has to have lived with the applicants for at least 10 weeks before the order may be applied for. If a local authority adoption agency is planning adoption for a child outside the UK, it will have to seek a permanence order with authority to adopt before the prospective adopters apply for the s.59 order.

s.59 2007 Act; Foreign Adoption Regs 2009

15

General local authority duties to children

1 Local authority

"Local authority" is defined in the 1995 and 2007 Acts as meaning the whole local authority and all its departments, not just the social work department. It means that the various departments within the local authority are obliged to carry out responsibilities, duties, etc.

The 2011 Act does not have a specific definition of the words "local authority", but it should be taken to mean the same as in the 1995 Act. In addition, all children who are subject to compulsory supervision order are "looked after" in terms of the 1995 Act, so its definition applies.

s.93(1) 1995 Act; s.119(1) 2007 Act; s.17(6) 1995 Act as amended by Schedule 5, para 2(4) 2011 Act

This chapter deals with the general duties of local authorities to all children in their area, and in particular towards children "in need". These provisions are concerned with what is generally seen as preventive work. Local authority duties to "looked after" children are dealt with in Chapter 16.

2 General welfare duty

Local authorities are under a statutory duty to promote social welfare generally for all people in their area, by giving advice, guidance and assistance. Under these provisions, they may give assistance in kind to children and families, and in cash and kind to those over 18, although there are some restrictions under the immigration legislation.

s.12 1968 Act amended by Schedule 4, para 15(11) 1995 Act

3 Wellbeing duties and GIRFEC

The 2014 Act amends the 1995 Act by inserting a new s.23A. There are a number of provisions that affect local authorities' duties and powers to children in their area, when they are owed to children and families, whether the children are "in need", "looked after", who are likely to be looked after, have been looked after or requiring other services. It includes a definition of wellbeing.

4 GIRFEC

Getting it Right for Every Child is now a statutory imperative on local authorities. Local authorities must carry out their duties to and provide services for children in such a way as to 'safeguard, support and promote their [children's] wellbeing'.

This lists the eight indicators of wellbeing used in the GIRFEC policies. These indicators are referred to by the acronym SHANARRI – Safe, Healthy, Achieving, Nurtured, Active, Respected, Responsible and Included.

s.96 2014 Act

5 Adoption Services Plans

When Children's Services Plans were introduced under the 1995 Act, the range of services to be covered included local authorities' adoption provision. However, the 2007 Act introduced a specific duty on local authorities to prepare plans about the adoption services they provide in their areas. These adoption plans may be prepared separately from overall Children's Services Plans or included in them.

s.4 2007 Act

6 Children's Services Planning – Part 3 2014 Act

The 2014 Act repealed and replaced aspects of the 1995 and 2007 Acts in relation to Children's Services Planning.

7 Duty to co-ordinate

The Act placed a duty on public bodies, including local authorities, to co-ordinate the planning, design and delivery of services for children and young people with a focus on improving wellbeing outcomes, and report collectively on how they are improving those outcomes.

8 Planning and preparation

Every three years, the local authority and relevant Health Board must prepare a Children's Service Plan relating to the aims and outcomes of the plan. The plan will cover corporate parents and services 'capable of having a significant effect on the wellbeing of children' and extends the existing duty to co-operate to all those consulted about the new children's services plan.

Other service providers whose function is to provide a service must comply with a request made of them by the local authority or health board to provide information, advice or assistance to help them exercise their functions.

9 Enforcement

Services must be provided in accordance with the children's services plan. If a local authority or health board does not comply with the planning requirements or with Ministerial guidance about these plans, then Scottish Ministers can transfer their children's services planning functions to other health boards or local authorities or require joint boards to be established for the purpose of planning services to consideration of the Children and Young People Act.

s.17 2014 Act

10 Duty to publish

The annual report on the plan should review the extent to which those services safeguard, support and promote the wellbeing of children in an integrated and efficient manner. It will also need to show how services have met outcomes set by Scottish Ministers in regulations.

11 Children "in need"

11.1

The 1995 Act introduced a definition of children in need as being children for whom as wide a range as possible of services should be provided, to promote their welfare and to assist them to develop. The main provision is in s.22 of the 1995 Act, but that section did not replace the general duty to do preventive work in s.12 of the 1968 Act. In practice, local authorities use their powers to provide services to children in need.

s.22 1995 Act

11.2

Local authorities must safeguard and promote the welfare of children in their area who are in need. These services may be in cash or kind.

The services provided under this duty may be for:

- the child; or
- their family, if the services help the child; or
- any other member of the family, if the services help the child.

s.22(1) and (3) 1995 Act

11.3

The definition of "in need" is very wide, and each local authority must have instructions and guidance so that individual decisions can be made about children and families. A child will be considered in need if they are:

- unlikely to achieve or maintain or have the opportunity of achieving or maintaining a reasonable standard of health or development unless they receive services; or
- their health or development is likely significantly to be impaired or further impaired unless services are provided; or
- they are disabled; or
- they are adversely affected by the disability of any other person in the family; or
- they are at risk of becoming a looked after child because they are not in a settled situation.

s.93(4)(a) 1995 Act

12 Disabled children and children affected by disability

The definition of "in need" includes children who are adversely affected by the disability of someone else in the family, as well as children who are themselves disabled. It refers also to children who act as carers for others in the family. The duties about carers' assessments apply to child carers as well as to adult ones.

s.24 1995 Act as amended by s.11(1) Community Care & Health (Scotland) Act 2002

13 Definition of disability

A person, including a child, is considered to be disabled if they have a physical or mental impairment and the impairment has a substantial and long-term adverse effect on their ability to perform normal day-to-day activities.

s.5 2010 Act

14 Child with disability

It includes children and young people with a comprehensive range of physical, emotional, developmental, learning, communication and health care needs. A child may be affected by the impairment of a family member if one of their parents or siblings is disabled. Disabled children are defined as "a child in need".

s.93(4) 1995 Act; s.23(2) 1995 Act as amended by Schedule 4, para 7 2003 Act

15 Duty of local authority to assess

Where a child is in need because of disability or affected by the impairment of a family member, the parents or guardians may ask for an assessment of the child or anyone else in the family, to establish the child's needs so far as attributable to the disability. The local authority must carry out this assessment if it is requested. It must take account of the views of the child, the parents and any carer who is providing "substantial" care to the disabled person; and take account of the "substantial" care when that is provided. When a local authority provides services to a child who is disabled or affected by the impairment of a family member, it should aim to help the child live as normal a life as possible.

s.23(3) and (4) 1995 Act, the latter inserted by the Community Care and Health (Scotland) Act 2002, s.10

16 Assessment of carer

Anyone providing substantial care for a disabled child (including another child) can also ask for a carer's assessment of their ability to provide the care. The local authority must carry out this assessment if it considers that the child should or may receive services as a child in need. When a child is in need because they are disabled, and the carer is providing substantial care, the local authority must tell them about being entitled to a carer's assessment.

s.24(1) and (1A), and s.24A 1995 Act, inserted by the Community Care and Health (Scotland) Act 2002, s.11

17 Self-directed support

Where the local authority has assessed the child and their family as needing support services, it must offer them a variety of options for deciding what support services they want and how they should be organised. Self-directed support service options are:

- to receive a direct payment from the local authority, so that the child or their family can arrange and manage the support themselves.
- to choose the type of support required but the local authority makes the arrangements and manages the budget.
- to ask the local authority to make the decisions about the type of support required, make the arrangements and manage the budget.
- a mix of three options.

Social Care (Self-Directed Support) (Scotland) Act 2013

18 Day care for children in need

When a child is in need, the local authority has a duty to provide day care for that child:

- during the day if the child is under five; or
- after school *and* during holidays if the child is of school age.

See Chapter 6 for general arrangements about day care. Day care can be provided by the local authority directly or by voluntary or independent agencies registered with the local authority. Care could be provided in a centre or by a childminder.

s.27 1995 Act

19 Local authority duty to consult representative parents

At least every two years, the local authority must consult "representative" parents of children in need and children not in need, about how these services should be provided. It must then publish its plans for delivery of these services.

s.27 1995 Act as amended by s.55 2014 Act

20 Early learning and child care

The 2014 Act imposes a duty on every 'education authority', (i.e. a local authority's education service), to provide 'early learning and childcare' for 'each eligible pre-school child' in their area. A child will be 'eligible' if they:

- are under school age, and
- have not started ordinary primary school, and
  - are aged two or over and is looked after), or
  - are aged two or over and are the subject of a kinship care order, or
  - are otherwise specified in secondary legislation.

An education authority may provide alternative arrangements for an 'eligible' looked after child in certain situations.

ss.68–70 2014 Act

21 Children at risk of being looked after

The 2014 Act also requires every local authority to provide 'relevant services' for children in their area who are at risk of being looked after or otherwise fit other descriptions in secondary legislation. Services involve providing information, advice, counselling or taking other actions, which may include payments. The duties extend to parents of such children and to pregnant women and their partners when expected children are likely to be looked after.

ss.68–70 2014 Act

16

Local authority responsibilities for "looked after" children

This chapter deals with looked after children, who they are, and what responsibilities local authorities have.

1 "Looked after" children

Looked after children is the term that was introduced by the 1995 Act and replaced references to children "in care". The definition of a looked after child is wider than the various definitions of "in care" and is different from the definitions in the law for England and Wales.

2 Who are looked after children?

2.1

Children are looked after if they are:

- accommodated by a local authority under s.25 of the 1995 Act, that is, accommodated on a voluntary basis;
- subject to compulsory supervision orders or interim compulsory supervision orders made by children's hearings under the 2011 Act (see Chapter 11);
- living in Scotland and subject to orders giving Scottish local authorities responsibilities, after transfers of orders under the Children (Reciprocal

Enforcement of Prescribed Orders etc (England and Wales and Northern Ireland) (Scotland) Regulations 1996, SI 1996/3267, made under s.33 of the 1995 Act; or Children's Hearings (Scotland) Act 2011 (Transfer of Children to Scotland – Effect of Orders made in England and Wales or Northern Ireland) Regulations 2013, SSI 2013/99, made under s.190 of the 2011 Act;

- subject to permanence orders and permanence orders with authority to adopt made under s.80 of the 2007 Act, including deemed permanence orders, which were formerly parental responsibilities orders (PROs) under s.86 of the 1995 Act.

In practical terms, children may be looked after in many different ways, including at home, in foster care, in kinship care, with prospective adopters, in residential placements and in secure accommodation.

s.17(6) (as amended by the 2007 and 2011 Acts), s.25 and s.33 1995 Act; s.80 2007 Act; ss.91, 119 and 190 2011 Act

2.2

If the authority for the placement or keeping of a child is not in this list, the child is not looked after. The list does not include a child who:

- is accommodated by virtue purely of educational placements; or
- is accommodated in a refuge provided under s.38 of the 1995 Act; or
- is the subject of a child arrangements order, child protection order or exclusion order.

However, when a child is the subject of a child protection order requiring the child to be removed to a place of safety, the local authority has the same duties towards the child as if they are looked after.

s.17(6) as amended 1995 Act; s.44 2011 Act

3 Duties of the local authority

3.1

There are a wide variety of duties owed by the local authority to looked after children. These duties are contained in the 1995 Act and the various regulations made thereunder, particularly the LAC Regulations 2009 and the Leaving Care Regs 2003. The guidance to the 2007 Act is also important.

ss.17 and 29–31 1995 Act, as amended and added to by the 2014 Act; LAC Regs 2009; Leaving Care Regs 2003; 2007 Act Guidance

3.2

The local authority duties listed in the 1995 Act are amended by the 2014 Act. The duties are to:

- safeguard and promote the child's welfare as paramount concern;
- safeguard, support and protect the child's wellbeing;
- make such use of services for the child as reasonable parents would;
- promote regular personal relations and direct contact between the child and anyone with parental responsibilities, having regard to the child's welfare as paramount and what is practical and appropriate;
- provide advice and assistance to a child, with a view to preparing them for when they are no longer looked after;
- find out and take account of the views of the child, their parents and others with responsibilities and rights or an interest in the child, before making any decisions about the child;
- take account of the child's religious persuasion, racial origin and cultural and linguistic background before making any decisions;
- carry out a review of each child's case at set intervals; and

- provide advice, guidance and assistance to any child who was looked after at the date on which they could leave school, is no longer looked after by a local authority and is under 19 – these duties are changed by the 2014 Act – see Chapter 9.

s.17(1)–(4), s.23A, s.31, s.29 1995 Act as amended by 2001 and 2014 Acts and s.29A

3.3

Further details of these and other duties are contained in the LAC Regs 2009 referred to above. There are some differences in the provisions as between children who are looked after and remain at home with their parents and those who are looked after away from their parents, with foster carers, kinship carers, in residential placements or with carers who have some PRRs under a permanence order or permanence order with authority to adopt. The LAC Regs 2009 cover a range of matters, including:

- what information has to be gathered and assessments made before or when children are looked after;
- that before or when children become looked after, there must be a written assessment of their health and need for health care;
- what requires to be in children's plans for all looked after children;
- notification of the death of looked after children;
- arrangements for different types of care for looked after children;
- notifications of placements;
- emergency placement arrangements;
- how and when children's cases are to be reviewed; and
- maintenance of case records for looked after children.

LAC Regs 2009, Regs 1–14, 27–30; 34–49

3.4

The provisions about reviews in the LAC Regulations 2009 are in two separate regulations for two different groups of looked after children. Regulation 44 covers children looked after and cared for by their parents or by other people who have parental responsibilities and rights (PRRs). This will include carers who have PRRs under permanence orders or permanence orders with authority to adopt. Regulation 45 covers children looked after and "placed" with kinship carers, foster carers, emergency carers (Reg 39(1)) or residential establishments. Regulation 45 includes children who have "respite" placements – see Chapter 9. However, neither regulation mentions children who are looked after under compulsory supervision orders or interim compulsory supervision orders which name carers who are not parents, have no PRRs and are not approved kinship or foster carers. For these children, Reg 45 should be used, as Reg 44 clearly does not apply.

LAC Regs 2009, Regs 44 and 45

4 Review of child's case: child cared for by parents or persons with parental responsibilities and parental rights

The frequency of reviews is not fixed automatically. The local authority has to discuss how often reviews will be held with individual children (depending on age and maturity) and carers. If there is no agreement about frequency, there must be a review within six weeks of placement, and at least every 12 months thereafter.

LAC Regs 2009, Reg 44

5 Review of the child's case: child placed with kinship carer, foster carer or in a residential establishment

Under Reg 45 there is a fixed structure of timescales for reviews, with some slight differences, depending on how children came into the care system and are looked after. Reviews for most children must be within six weeks of the placement; then within a further three months; and then within every six months thereafter. Children who are looked after because respite care is provided only need to have reviews three months after the first placement, and then within every six months thereafter.

LAC Regs 2009, Reg 45

6 Provision of accommodation

Local authorities have a duty to accommodate children for whom no one has parental responsibilities, or who are lost or abandoned, or who cannot be cared for by their normal carers, temporarily or permanently, for whatever reason. Such care is often referred to as "voluntary" care, as it comes about by agreement with parents or carers, or a complete absence of any parents or carers, not because of an order from a court or hearing. The local authority must provide such accommodation for children up to 18 where they fall into the above categories. Children accommodated in this way are looked after and placed.

s.25 1995 Act

7 Short breaks

This term is not specifically mentioned in the 1995 Act or the LAC Regs 2009, but the effect of these is that all short break placements that are planned by local authorities and that last for more than 24 hours at a time are treated as looked after placements in terms of s.25 arrangements – provision of accommodation. Such arrangements are therefore regulated and the children are treated as looked after and placed children. This includes children with disabilities for whom such respite short breaks are provided. If short breaks are provided in family homes as opposed to residential establishments, the carers must be foster carers or kinship carers approved in terms of the LAC Regs 2009. A series of short break placements can be treated as a single placement subject to certain conditions. The first review must be within three months of the first placement; and only one medical assessment is needed at the beginning, not every time a child receives short break care.

LAC Regs 2009, Reg 14 (kinship care) and 30 (foster care) and 45(3)

8 Continuing care and after care for previously looked after children

Local authorities have duties to certain young people when they cease to be looked after where they were looked after on their 16th birthday.

8.1 Continuing care

Local authorities have a duty to provide "continuing care" for formerly looked after young people, from the age of 16. This will allow them to remain living in their accommodation even though they are no longer looked after up to the age of 21.

This will not apply where:

- I. *the accommodation was secure,*
- II. *carer has indicated to the authority that they are unable or unwilling to continue to provide the placement.*
- III. *if the young person leaves the accommodation of their own volition*
- IV. *or the local authority considers that providing the care would significantly adversely affect the welfare of the person.*

A young person receiving continuing care cannot also receive aftercare support at the same time. Once continuing care ceases, the young person can apply for after care support.

Part 11 2014 Act

8.2 After care

An application for assessment for after care can be made to the local authority by a child looked after on their 16th birthday. Where the local authority identifies an "eligible need", it will provide the child with support and this can continue up until they are 26. This can be:

- financial support for accommodation;
- information and advice to access education, training, employment and skills-related opportunities;
- information, advice, guidance and assistance if the local authority considers it necessary to meet the child's needs as regards their welfare where these cannot otherwise be met.

Part 10 2014 Act

Further reading

Books and publications

Adoption Policy Review Group (2005) *Adoption: Better choices for our children – Report of Phase II,* Edinburgh: Scottish Executive. Available on the Scottish Government website, under Publications, 29 June 2005.

Butterworths (1997 onwards) *Scottish Family Law Service*, London: Butterworths/LexisNexis. This is a loose-leaf publication, updated every six months.

Disclosure Scotland (2012) *Updated Guidance on Foster Care, Kinship Care and Adoption*. Available from www.disclosurescotland.co.uk – click on Publications.

Green (1997 onwards) *Scottish Family Law Legislation and Scottish Social Work Legislation*, Edinburgh: W Green/Thomson. These are annotated statutes, etc, published in loose-leaf form and updated regularly.

McNeill PGB and Morag J (2010) *Adoption of Children in Scotland* (4th edition), Edinburgh: W Green/Sweet & Maxwell

Morrison M (2021) *Effective Adoption and Fostering Panels in Scotland*, London: CoramBAAF

Norrie K McK (2004) *Children (Scotland) Act 1995 – Annotated version* (2nd edition), Edinburgh: W Green/Sweet & Maxwell

Norrie K McK (2013) *Children's Hearings in Scotland* (3rd edition), Edinburgh: W Green/Sweet & Maxwell

Plumtree A (2003) *Choices for Children*, Edinburgh: Scottish Executive for the

Adoption Policy Review Group. Available on the Scottish Government website under Publications, 11 September 2003.

The Scottish Executive (2004) *Supporting Young People Leaving Care in Scotland: Regulations and guidance on services for young people ceasing to be looked after by local authorities*, Edinburgh: TSO. Available on the Scottish Government website under Publications, 31 March 2004.

The Scottish Executive (2005) *Secure and Safe Homes for our Most Vulnerable Children: Scottish Executive proposals for action on the APRG Phase II Report*, Edinburgh: Scottish Executive. Available on the Scottish Government website under Publications, 30 June 2005.

The Scottish Government (2010) *National Guidance for Child Protection in Scotland 2010*, Edinburgh: Scottish Government. Available on the Scottish Government website under Publications, 13 December 2010. It has been amended and added to and will be issued in a refreshed version in early 2014.

The Scottish Government (2011) *Guidance on the Looked After Children (Scotland) Regulations 2009 and the Adoption and Children (Scotland) Act 2007*, Edinburgh: Scottish Government. Available on the Scottish Government website under Publications, 10 March 2011.

The Scottish Government (2013) *Private Fostering in Scotland: Practice guidance for local authority children's services,* Edinburgh: Scottish Government. Available on the Scottish Government website under Publications, 29 November 2013.

The Scottish Office (1997) *Scotland's Children: The Children (Scotland) Act 1995, Regulations and Guidance: Volume 1: Support and protection for children and their families,* Edinburgh: HMSO. Available on the Scottish Government website under Publications, 12 October 2004.

Thomson JM (2011) *Family Law in Scotland* (6th edition), Edinburgh: Bloomsbury

Wilkinson A and Norrie K McN (2013) *Parent and Child* (3rd edition Norrie K McN), Edinburgh: W Green

Useful websites

AFKA Scotland
www.afkascotland.org

Supports practitioners and organisations working in fostering, kinship and adoption. Provides training, resources and information.

Care Inspectorate
www.careinspectorate.com/

Responsible for the regulation, registration and inspection of Scottish care services. There is a link on the Home page to the National Care Standards.

CELCIS, Centre of Excellence for Looked After Children in Scotland
www.celcis.org/

Children's Hearings Scotland, CHS
www.chscotland.gov.uk/

Responsible for panel members for the children's hearing system, including recruitment, training, support and monitoring.

COPFS, Crown Office and Procurator Fiscal Service
www.crownoffice.gov.uk/

Responsible for criminal prosecutions in Scotland.

CoramBAAF
www.corambaaf.org.uk

Membership organisation for professionals working across adoption, fostering and kinship. Provides publications, training and advice.

Department for Education intercountry adoption website
www.gov.uk/guidance/intercountry-adoption-information-for-adoption-agencies

The DfE is responsible for adoption in England. The information about countries and adopting from them is helpful, but the legal input should be treated with caution, as many provisions are different in Scotland.

Disclosure Scotland
www.mygov.scot/disclosure-types

Information Commissioner for the UK
www.informationcommissioner.gov.uk/

Responsible for monitoring DPA 1998 and also for FOI for public authorities.

Coram Intercountry Adoption Centre
www.coramiac.org.uk/

Safeguarders Panel
www.childrenfirst.org.uk/get-support/our-services/safeguarders-panel/

Children 1st manages the Safeguarders Panel, part of the children's hearing system. There is information under 'Our services' on the Children 1st website.

Scottish Children's Reporter Administration, SCRA
www.scra.gov.uk/

SCRA is responsible for the reporters' service in the children's hearing system.

Scottish Courts Service
www.scotcourts.gov.uk/

Scottish Government
www.gov.scot/

Scottish Government Intercountry Adoption
www.gov.scot/policies/looked-after-children/adoption/

Scottish Information Commissioner
www.foi.scot/

The Commissioner is responsible for FOI for Scottish public authorities.

Scottish Throughcare and Aftercare Forum
www.staf.scot/

UK Border Agency
www.gov.uk/government/organisations/uk-visas-and-immigration

For information about intercountry adoption, use the search function.

Specific online resources

Court Rules online
www.scotcourts.gov.uk/rules-and-practice/rules-of-court/court-of-session-rules/

All the Scottish court rules are available on the Scottish Courts website.

Sheriff Court Practice Notes online
www.scotcourts.gov.uk/rules-and-practice/practice-notes-and-directions#/

Sheriff Court Practice Notes are issued from time to time by individual Sheriffs Principal for their Sheriffdom, and are available on the Scottish Courts website. They are listed by year and by Sheriffdom. Those for proceedings under the Adoption and Children (Scotland) Act 2007 were all published in 2009.

Judgments online
www.scotcourts.gov.uk/judgments/#/

Judgements in Court of Session cases and some sheriff court cases, from September 1998 onwards, are available on the Scottish Courts website.

Legislation online
www.legislation.gov.uk/

All Acts, regulations, orders and court rules are available on this website.

'Browse' at www.legislation.gov.uk/explore and the page shows all types of legislation, which can be accessed by the relevant link. These include:

- UK Public Acts, made at Westminster
- Acts of the Scottish Parliament
- Scottish Statutory Instruments, SSIs, including court rules
- Statutory Instruments, SIs